BEADING
BASICS

BEADING BASICS

All you need to know to create
beautiful beaded accessories

Stephanie Burnham

BARRON'S

A QUARTO BOOK

Copyright © 2006 Quarto Inc.

First edition for the United States, its territories
and dependencies, and Canada published in 2006
by Barron's Educational Series, Inc.

All inquiries should be addressed to:
Barron's Educational Series, Inc.
250 Wireless Boulevard
Hauppauge, NY 11788
www.barronseduc.com

Library of Congress Catalog Card Number:
2005929079

ISBN-13: 978-0-7641-5921-3
ISBN-10: 0-7641-5921-6

Conceived, designed, and produced by
Quarto Publishing plc
The Old Brewery
6 Blundell Street
London N7 9BH

QUA: BEAB

Editor: Michelle Pickering
Art editor: Julie Joubinaux
Designer: Jon Wainwright
Photographer: Phil Wilkins
Illustrator: Kate Simunek
Indexer: Dorothy Frame
Assistant art director: Penny Cobb

Art director: Moira Clinch
Publisher: Paul Carslake

Color separation by Provision Pte Ltd, Singapore
Printed by Star Standard Industries Pte Ltd, Singapore

9 8 7 6 5 4 3 2 1

CONTENTS

INTRODUCTION

The purpose of this book is both to instruct and to inspire you to create your own beaded jewelry and accessories. Complete beginners who have not previously picked up a bead or beading needle will find projects that are easy to work and stylish to wear. More experienced beaders will find ideas that will encourage them to take their work in new directions.

The book starts with an overview of the tools and materials you will need. You will be happy to discover that a beading needle, some beading thread, and a selection of beads are enough to get going, so even a complete novice can give beadwork a try without having to purchase lots of expensive items. Supplies of beads, tools, findings, wires, and threads are readily available from bead stores, mail-order services, and online bead suppliers (you will find a list of resources on page 124). This chapter also provides some guidance on how to mix and match colors to create pleasing results.

Then comes the heart of the book: the techniques and projects. This chapter has been organized so that you learn the different techniques of beadwork progressively. The first few pages of each section are devoted to a particular beadwork technique, explaining the basic technique and providing useful variations. These pages are followed by two or more projects that use the basic technique you have just learned. What better or more rewarding way to master the technique than to practice it by making beautiful beaded jewelry.

Both the techniques and the projects are written clearly and concisely, with enlarged step-by-step photographs that are easy to comprehend and that will quickly inspire confidence. Some steps also have close-up "satellite" photos, so you can see a particular step through from beginning to end. There are also a few techniques that are used in most beadwork pieces, such as starting and finishing off threads, plus ideas for embellishments to give your pieces that final touch.

From learning about what materials to work with and how to attach clasps to threading a bead loom and adding a fringe, this book will give you a superb grounding in the craft of beadwork. Once you have discovered how fantastic working with beads can be, you will soon have the confidence to adapt and experiment with the techniques to create stunning pieces of beadwork that are uniquely your own.

TOOLS AND MATERIALS

When you first become interested in working with beads and start to look around in specialty bead stores and on the Internet, it soon becomes apparent that there is a huge range of tools and materials available. Buying at this stage without knowing exactly what you need can be costly and result in your buying items unnecessarily. Start by looking through the projects in this book and decide which you would like to tackle first. Then you can arm yourself with a small shopping list before you make any purchases. Start with a small selection and build up your collection gradually. As far as beads are concerned, a good rule of thumb is to buy what appeals to you—you can be sure that at some point you will incorporate them into your designs.

Another important thing to consider when starting beadwork is where you are going to work. Good lighting is essential because some beads are very small. You may even need a magnifying glass to ensure that you do not strain your eyes. A good chair is also important, as well as a work surface that is at the correct height so that you do not lean over and strain your back. Getting your working environment right will make your beading all the more enjoyable.

Beads

Beads are available in such a huge range of shapes, sizes, colors, and designs that the choice can seem overwhelming at first. When purchasing beads, buy the best quality you can afford. Try to avoid cheap beads because they may be misshapen or break easily, so you could end up discarding more than you use. They may also have sharp, uneven edges that can cause the beading thread to break and so ruin a piece of beadwork.

Seed beads

The term seed bead refers to any small bead. Usually made of glass, the most common type is round, but triangle, cube, and cylinder seed beads are also popular and widely available. They work well in most beadweaving techniques, and are also used as decorative spacers between accent beads. Whenever the generic term *seed bead* is used, both throughout this book and in beadwork in general, it is the round seed beads that are being referred to. Seed beads are produced in Japan, the Czech Republic, India, China, and France, and are commonly sold by gram weight.

◄▼ Bugle beads
These long, cylindrical tubes are available in several sizes, including 4 and 6 mm. Most seed beads are "tumbled" in the factory to smooth the edges, but bugles are not because they would break. They start life as long tubes of glass that are cut to the correct lengths. This means that they can have sharp edges, so always check bugles before incorporating them into your design. Discard any sharp-edged beads because they will cut the beading thread and ruin your beadwork. Cheaper bugles, in particular, tend to be quite badly cut, but even the best-quality Japanese bugles need to be checked carefully before use.

◄► Round beads
Usually referred to simply as seed beads, these small round beads are also known as rocaille. They are available in a variety of sizes, including 6, 8, 11, and 15 mm, and in many different colors and finishes. Their round, polished shape means that these beads blend and mold together well, making them ideal for all beadweaving techniques.

◄ ► Triangle beads

Triangle beads are available in a variety of sizes, including 5, 8, and 10 mm, and in a wide range of colors and finishes. Although the beads are triangular, the hole through the center is usually round. Triangle beads mold together very well, almost like the scales of an animal, and give added shape and texture to a design.

▼ ► Japanese cylinder beads

Often referred to by their brand names— Miyuki Delicas, Toho Treasures, and Toho Aiko—these small cylindrical beads have an extra-large hole through the center. They are extremely high in quality, and are among the most regular, uniform beads available in the world today. These beads mold together beautifully, making them ideal for pictorial or patterned beadwork.

◄ ► Cube beads

Cube beads are square, usually with a round hole through the center. The most commonly used and widely available size is 4 mm. They are available in a wide variety of colors, and help to give strength and stability to a design.

THE CUFF OF THIS CHARM BRACELET (PROJECT 11) IS MADE FROM ROUND SEED BEADS INTERSPERSED WITH CUBE BEADS, WHILE TWO STYLES OF FLOWER ACCENT BEADS FORM THE CHARMS.

ACCENT BEADS

Along with seed beads, the projects in this book also feature accent beads. This term is used to refer to any beads that stand out from the seed beads as a special feature of the design. These include faceted crystals, drop beads, shells, flowers, stars, and charms, and are made of a variety of materials, from glass to metal. Glass accent beads are available in the greatest variety of shapes, colors, and sizes, and come from many different countries around the world, including India, China, Italy, and the Czech Republic. There is also a multitude of plastic beads, from inexpensive, brightly colored children's beads to collectable plastics such as Bakelite. Other materials used to make beads include metal, wood, shell, ceramic, and semiprecious stones.

◄ Glass-blown beads
These glass beads are handblown individually, often with surface decoration added afterward. They tend to be more expensive because the beads are made one at a time.

▼ Austrian crystal beads
The famous Swarovski company in Austria has been producing these popular crystal beads for many years.

► Dichroic beads
Dichroic glass is especially made for glass artists producing their own glass beads.

◄ Czech Republic beads
These accent beads are made from special pattern molds passed down through generations of families.

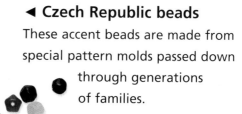

▼ ▶ Plastic beads

There are plenty of inexpensive, cheerful plastic beads available, and good-quality plastic beads can easily be mistaken for glass ones. It is not until you pick one up and feel the lightness of it that you realize it is made from plastic.

▼ Metalized plastic beads

These plastic beads are covered in a very durable plastic coating in different metallic finishes.

▼ ▶ Metal beads

Metal beads are available in highly prized metals such as gold and silver as well as base metals such as copper, brass, and aluminum. They are produced around the world, including Thailand, India, and Bali. Many countries also make ranges of plated metal beads.

▼ Shell and pearl beads

Whole or sliced shells and pearls, available with pre-drilled holes, can be threaded into many beadwork designs. Their iridescence is perfect for making eye-catching pieces of jewelry.

Tools

Many of the tools used for beadworking can be bought from your local hardware store, craft store, or if you are lucky enough to have one nearby, bead supplier. Also check the Internet and the resources on page 124. For many of the beadwork techniques featured in this book, the only essential tools are a needle and scissors. Purchase additional equipment, such as pliers for wirework, as you progress.

◄ Beading needles

Beading needles are available in both long and short lengths. Long needles are easier for beginners to work with for most beadwork techniques, but short needles (sometimes called sharps) are easier for netting stitch. Needles are also available in different thicknesses. The size you use will be determined by the size of the beads, the type of thread, and the stitch being used. As a general guide, size 10 needles are suitable for most beadwork projects, while size 13 needles are great for loomwork and square stitch, when a slightly finer needle is required.

► Scissors

A small, sharp pair of scissors is essential for cutting thread ends cleanly and evenly.

▲ Beading mat

A beading mat is not essential, but it does make working with beads easier. The mat is made of a soft, foamlike material so that the beads sit right on top of it but will not roll around, making them easy to pick up with a needle without the needle getting caught in any pile. It also allows you to have all the beads you are using out at once instead of having to keep opening and closing bead containers.

▼ Beading loom

Looms are available in several forms, from inexpensive plastic versions to expandable looms made from the best-quality wood. It is a good idea to start with an inexpensive loom to see if you enjoy this type of beadwork. If you do, you can invest in a more expensive good-quality loom later. Looms are available from most craft and bead stores, but you could always improvise and build your own using a wooden rectangle and nails.

◀ Round nose pliers

These pliers have smooth, round "noses" that are used to shape wire into loops and rings. A pair with neat, short noses is best because they will allow you to make small, neat loops and maintain good control of the work.

▶ Chain nose pliers

These pliers have pointed noses that are round on the outside and flat on the inside. They are used for opening and closing small chain links, as well as for tucking in ends of wire in tight places.

▲ Cutting pliers

These do what their name says: they cut wire. If you are using memory wire, you will need heavy-duty cutters or special memory wire cutters.

▲ Flat nose pliers

These pliers have flat ends that are useful for holding wire and bending it at angles. They can hold several strands of wire securely and are also useful for closing jump rings.

◀ Flush cutters

These allow you to cut wire absolutely flush to your work. They have small, neat, pointed ends that will go into small spaces.

FINDINGS

Strictly speaking, the term *findings* refers to all the components used to make a piece of jewelry. However, most people use it to refer to the mechanical parts that are used to assemble the jewelry—for example, earring wires and clasps. These findings are often decorative as well as functional. Using the right findings for the piece you are making is very important, because it can mean the difference between a beautifully finished item and a spoiled one.

METALWORK FINDINGS

This first section describes findings that consist of the bits and pieces of metalwork used within the bead or wirework design; the second section on page 20 deals with the various clasps and fastenings available. Most findings are available in plated or pure metals, in silver or gold colors. It is advisable to use sterling silver or gold for earwires.

◀ Ear posts and ear wires

Ear posts are straight pieces of wire that fit directly into a pierced ear. Ear wires are a shepherd's crook shape that slides through the hole in the ear. Both types are available with a small loop at the front to which you can attach the main body of the earring.

◀ Ear nuts

These fit onto the back of ear posts to hold the earrings securely in place.

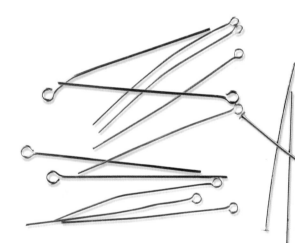

▲ Eyepins and headpins

These are used as a support for beads when creating earrings. Headpins are also used to attach beads and charms to a chain bracelet. Headpins look like small nails, with the flat head of the pin preventing the beads from falling off. Eyepins have a small loop of wire at the head of the pin, from which you can dangle a drop bead.

▲ Jump rings

These circles of metal are used either for linking pieces together or for attaching a fastener. They are easy to open and close using pliers.

▶ Split rings

These are double circles of metal that work just like the rings on the end of a keychain. They have the same uses as jump rings but are more secure.

▶ Flat leather crimps

Leather crimps are used to attach fasteners to cotton, leather, suede, or ribbon by clamping the thong between the crimps. The fastener is then attached to the loop at the end of the crimp for a truly professional finish.

◀ Clam shells and knot cups

These consist of two half spheres with a small loop at one end. The spheres are closed around the knot at the end of a string of beads and a fastener is attached to the loop. Clam shells, also known as calottes, cover the knot sideways; knot cups, also known as bead tips, have a hole between the two half-spheres through which the thread passes before it is tied into a knot.

▲ Cones and end caps

These are widely used to finish multistrand necklaces and bracelets. End caps come in a variety of shapes; cones are, obviously, conical.

◀ End bars

These are used to finish a multirow necklace or bracelet, with a fastening attached to the other side.

◀ Spacer bars

Spacer bars can be used to keep the strands separated on a multirow necklace or bracelet.

FASTENINGS AND CLASPS

There are numerous different types of fastenings and clasps available, in many shapes, sizes, and finishes. Remember that a good closure can really complement your design. Many people skimp on clasps, preferring a less expensive one that seems like a bargain, but unfortunately this often shows. Think of all the expense, time, and effort that went into creating your finished piece—isn't it worth finishing off well with a great clasp?

▶ Lobster clasps

Lobster clasps are discrete and tidy, and probably the most useful fastener to have in your stash. The lobster clasp is fitted to one end of the finished piece, with a jump ring or split ring opposite to fasten it to. These clasps look great on bracelets and necklaces, but if using the smaller sizes, they can be a little awkward to fasten on your own.

◀ Toggle clasps

A toggle clasp consists of a ring and a T-bar section, each with a looped fixing point for attaching the clasp to the finished item. Toggle clasps work well on necklaces and bracelets, and are quite easy to fasten. They are available in many sizes, from tiny to fairly large, but be careful not to use too big a toggle or it will detract from the design. Place the toggle alongside the piece first to check that it looks good.

◀ Magnetic clasps

Magnetic clasps are great for anyone with dexterity problems, because they often have quite strong magnets and stick together really well. They are available in many finishes, from sterling silver and gold to nickel-free plated. The problem with them is that they love to attach themselves to steel objects without your knowing. They are also unsuitable for people with pacemakers.

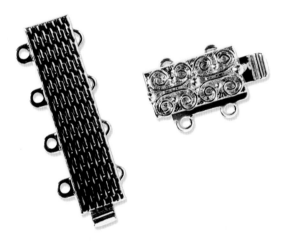

▲ Bar clasps

These come in two-, three-, four-, and five-bar sizes. They are a great help when creating cuff bracelets because, with several fixing points along the clasp for extra security, they hold the entire width of the bracelet in place.

▲ Hook and loop fasteners

The hook is attached to one side of the piece, with the loop on the other side. This type of fastener is easy to open and close but not as secure as some other clasp styles.

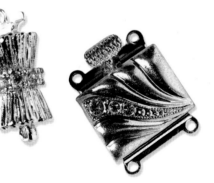

◄ Simple clasps

These clasps, including spring rings, box clasps, barrel clasps, and fish hook clasps, tend to be at the less expensive end of the market and usually have only one small fixing point at each side of the clasp. They are not always a good fit and can be very stiff for the first few uses. They are certainly not very easy to open for anyone with arthritis because they require a lot of pressure. However, if you are making jewelry for a bazaar or charity and you need to keep costs down, they will certainly help.

► Elaborate clasps

These clasps speak for themselves. They are nicely finished, with really good color and design. They would finish off any design perfectly and are well worth the initial outlay.

▲ Clamping clasps

This clasp has a large staplelike fastener at each end, together with a lobster clasp and chain extension for securing. The clasp is designed to clamp down onto the ends of wire knitting or ribbon, using flat nose pliers to secure it.

◄ Mesh pins and pin backs

Mesh pins have two pieces: a mesh section and a pin back. The mesh section can be decorated with beads and wire, then clamped onto the pin back. Pin backs can be sewn onto the back of a finished design that you wish to make into a pin.

COLOR THEORY

One of the most exciting features of beadworking is the impact of color, but many people who are new to the craft say that they find color really challenging, and there are so many beads to choose from that they feel overwhelmed. Some people seem to have more of an aptitude for color than others, but it is possible to learn how to use it to great effect by exploring the basic principles of color theory. Always remember, however, that color is a personal choice and that there are no hard-and-fast rules.

THE COLOR WHEEL

The relationship between different colors can be demonstrated on a color wheel showing the primary, secondary, and tertiary colors. The primary colors are red, yellow, and blue. The secondary colors sit between pairs of primaries and are made by mixing those two primary colors together. The secondary colors are orange (a mixture of yellow and red), green (a mixture of yellow and blue), and violet (a mixture

of blue and red). The tertiary colors sit between each pair of primary and secondary colors because they are produced by mixing those two colors together, making red-orange, yellow-orange, yellow-green, blue-green, blue-violet, and red-violet. Lighter tints can be created by adding white to each color. Darker shades can be created by adding black to each color.

COLOR QUALITIES

Colors that are opposite on the color wheel are called complementary, or contrasting; for example, blue and orange. They create vibrancy when placed next to each other. Colors that sit next to each other on the color wheel are called analogous, or harmonious; for example, yellow, yellow-orange, and orange. They produce a more subtle and harmonious effect when used together, because they each contain some of the same color.

Red

Red-orange

Red-violet

Orange

Violet

Yellow-orange

Blue-violet

Yellow

Blue

Yellow-green

Blue-green

Green

NEUTRALS

Neutral colors, such as white, black, cream, brown, and gray, do not appear as pure colors on the color wheel but are made by mixing pure colors together. For example, if an artist mixed pigments of all three primaries together in equal intensities, the result would be black. Mixing pigments of colors opposite each other on the color wheel produces a range of grays and browns. Neutrals, therefore, work well with all colors on the color wheel and can be used to great effect in beadwork, especially in backgrounds and to set off other colors.

VALUE AND TEMPERATURE

Other characteristics to keep in mind when choosing colors are whether their tonal value is light or dark and whether they are warm or cool colors. Reds and browns are generally warm colors, whereas blues and greens are cool. In general, warm colors tend to advance and cool colors tend to recede. The same is true with dark and light tones of the same color—dark tones tend to advance and light tones tend to recede.

TERMINOLOGY

Hue: The actual color on the wheel: red, blue, and green, for example.

Tint: Any hue with the addition of white to make the color paler.

Shade: A hue with the addition of black, or any other dark color to make it darker.

Tonal value: All tints and shades are tones of a color in relation to black or white. Tonal value describes the lightness or darkness of a color on a scale from white to black.

THIS BRACELET (PROJECT 5) IS MADE FROM SEED BEADS IN A SPECTRUM OF 12 COLORS. USE THE COLOR WHEEL TO HELP YOU SELECT YOUR PALETTE OF RAINBOW COLORS.

COLOR SCHEMES

When planning a project, it is a good idea to get out your bead tubes and experiment with putting different colors together. Many people choose colors based on a gut feeling, but it is often helpful to refer to a color wheel (page 22). Spend time sorting through your bead colors. By placing them on the wheel, you will soon see schemes coming together. Remember that you could always take a color wheel with you when purchasing beads. It will help you and ultimately stop you from making mistakes when selecting colors for a project.

ANALOGOUS SCHEME

These are colors, including tints and shades, that lie next to each other on the wheel. You can choose from two to six colors—a third of the complete color wheel. Be aware that if you choose an analogous color scheme and your beads are similar in tonal value, your project will look lovely but may lack impact. Adding a small amount of a complementary color to analogous colors— a touch of orange to blues and violets, for example—will provide sparkle.

COMPLEMENTARY SCHEME

Choosing colors that are opposite each other on the wheel will produce the greatest amount of contrast. Complementary colors may clash with each other when used at full strength, so try tints and shades. Alternatively, follow the 80:20 rule—that is, 80 percent of one color and 20 percent of the complementary color. If you use 50 percent of each color, they can fight and the result will not be as restful to look at.

MONOCHROMATIC SCHEME

Single-color, monochromatic schemes can work very well if you include beads of different shades and tints of the main color.

SAMPLE SCHEMES

Examine the color schemes used in the projects to see how different colors work together. You might like to try experimenting with your own beads to come up with alternative color schemes.

Project 1: Seashore bracelet

The shell embellishment was the starting point for this color scheme. There are browns, greens, and peaches within the shells, so a warm brown for the seed bead base is an appropriate choice. Green, peach, and matte brown are used in the branch fringing to give added texture and depth to the piece.

Project 17: Wirework charm bracelet

The gold chain works harmoniously with the different tones of green beads, while splashes of orange give the bracelet impact. However, if you choose a silver chain, you could try adding pinks, purples, or even a touch of black or crystal to produce a dramatic effect.

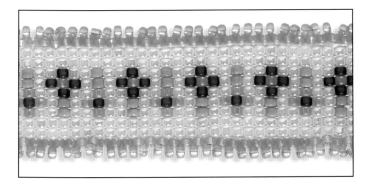

Project 12: Friendship bracelet

This design could be worked in almost any color scheme. Pearlized cream seed beads give the bracelet a fresh summer look, but you could choose to work the background in a much darker color to give a more dramatic impact to the design.

Project 14: Meteor shower bracelet

This monochromatic piece has a distinctly evening feel, with crystal beads down the spine to add sparkle and shine. The project could be given a very different look by using spring/summer colors for the base, with the addition of flower and leaf accent beads on the spine.

TECHNIQUES AND PROJECTS

This book has been created primarily for anyone who has ever thought about trying jewelry making but never had the confidence or found detailed enough instructions to make attempting it possible. Each of the techniques featured in the book has been split into small, easy-to-follow sections so that the technical step-by-step method of how to work the stitches is featured first, followed directly by two or more projects employing that particular technique. So, if you do get stuck, you only need to flip back one or two pages to remind yourself how to work a particular stitch.

Although this book explains beadwork right from the basics, the projects range from simple to more elaborate designs that will appeal to experienced beaders as well as to beginners. Even if you are already familiar with a technique, you may find some of the tips and step-by-step explanations useful. This chapter provides a taste of most of the main beadwork techniques and will hopefully inspire you to go on expanding your skills and discovering this wonderful and relaxing craft.

Technique: PEYOTE STITCH

Peyote stitch is one of the most versatile off-loom techniques, producing a flexible piece of beadwork that feels almost like fabric. The tension of the thread plays a major part in the appearance and texture of the stitch. A stop bead is used to prevent beads from falling off the tail end of the thread, as well as to tighten the tension of the beadwork. Peyote is best worked with a single strand of thread, but use two strands to create a firmer base for freestanding and three-dimensional beadwork.

EVEN-COUNT PEYOTE

For beginners, peyote stitch is easier to achieve with an even number of beads. An odd count involves maneuvering the needle and thread through several beads to arrive in the right place and direction to start the next row, so it should only be attempted once you have mastered working with an even count.

Getting the tension right

The first two or three rows of peyote stitch can be difficult to control because the beads move about a lot, so it is best to hold the rows between a thumb and forefinger rather than trying to bead on a table. To tighten the tension, pull the working end of the thread firmly in the direction you are beading. When the row is complete, use a thumbnail to push the stop bead toward the main beadwork.

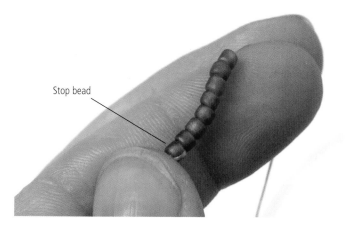

Stop bead

step 2 Thread on seven more beads, pulling the thread through so that all eight beads sit snugly together.

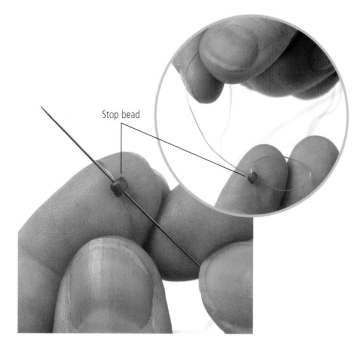

Stop bead

step 1 Thread a beading needle with 1 yd. (1 m) of beading thread. Slide a bead to within 6 in. (15 cm) of the tail end of the thread. Bring the needle back up through the bead to create a loop around the bead. This is called the stop bead.

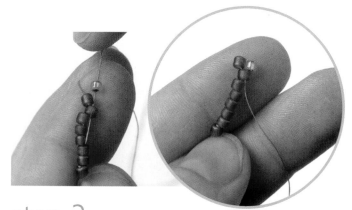

step 3 Holding all the threaded beads between a thumb and forefinger, pick up another bead with the needle, then take the needle through the next to last bead on the first row.

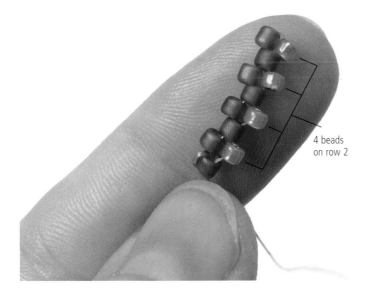

4 beads
on row 2

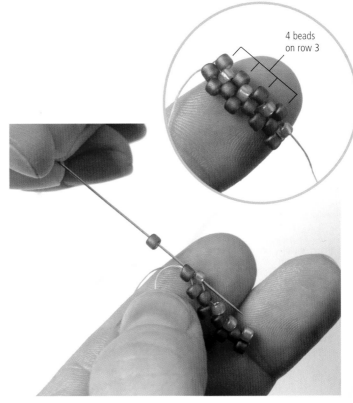

4 beads
on row 3

step 4 Continue along the row, taking the needle through every other bead, until you have added four beads. Two colors of beads are used here to make the different rows easy to see. Note the gaps between the beads on row 2. This is where you need to place the beads for the next row.

step 5 Pick up another bead with the needle to start row 3. Take the needle through the last bead added on row 2, which should be sitting slightly raised above the first row of beads. Continue in this way to the end of the row. You should have added four beads on row 3.

step 6 At this point, starting row 4, you may find it easier to flip the beadwork over as shown. Continue adding rows of beads until you are confident about working the stitch.

TWO-NEEDLE START

If you find starting peyote stitch a little difficult, you may find it easier to start with two needles instead of one.

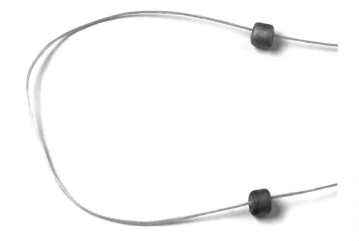

step 1 Thread a beading needle onto each end of a 1-yd. (1-m) length of beading thread. Pick up two beads, taking them down toward the middle of the looped thread.

step 2 Thread a third bead onto one of the needles, then pass the other needle through the same bead. Push the bead down toward the first two beads so that they sit one above the other, with the third bead sitting alongside both.

step 3 Pick up one bead with each needle and push them down toward the first three. Continue in this way until you have the required length of base. When you start the next row, revert to one needle and thread (see Even-count peyote, page 28). Leave the second thread to one side until your working thread runs out.

TUBULAR PEYOTE

Tubular peyote creates a hollow tube of beads and can be worked around any cylindrical object, such as a drinking straw, a piece of dowel, or a bottle. Beginners may find it helpful to use a cylinder made of transparent material so that the work can be seen clearly. If you start with an even number of beads, as demonstrated here, you will need to step up at the end of each row in order to move the needle up to the correct position for adding the next row. If using an odd number, you will automatically spiral up to the next row.

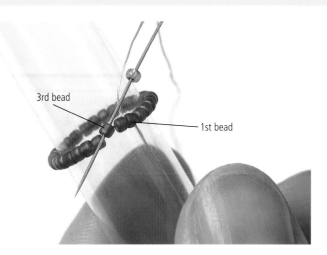

3rd bead

1st bead

step 3 Pick up another bead, then take the needle through the third bead along from the start of the first row. Pull slightly so that the new bead sits neatly on top of the second bead in row 1. Continue in this way until you arrive back at the first bead.

step 1 Thread an even number of beads onto the thread and tie it around a tubular object with a double knot, leaving a tiny gap between the first and last bead in the circle (do not overlap the beads or the stitch will not lie correctly and it will be impossible to work).

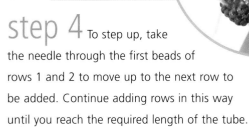

step 4 To step up, take the needle through the first beads of rows 1 and 2 to move up to the next row to be added. Continue adding rows in this way until you reach the required length of the tube.

step 2 Thread the needle and take it back through the first bead.

Technique: STARTING AND FINISHING THREADS

There are several ways to start and finish off threads, and everyone has their favorite. Some bead workers prefer not to make any knots, instead choosing to weave the ends backward and forward until the thread appears to be secure. Others prefer to tie a discrete knot, feeling that the beadwork seems more secure this way. Try different methods and work with the one that suits you best.

STARTING A THREAD

Always attach a new length of working thread before you finish off the old thread, because it can be difficult to see where the new thread needs to be positioned without the help of the old one.

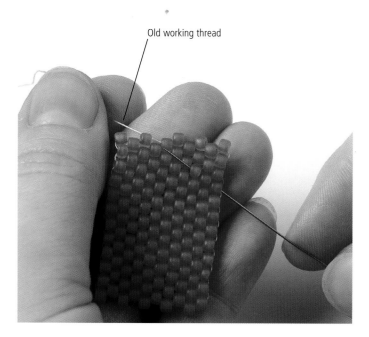

Old working thread

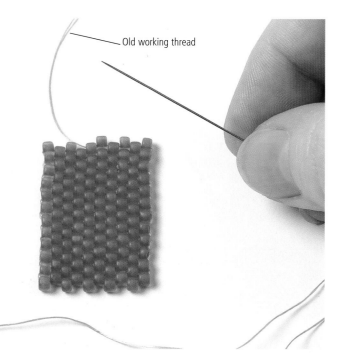

Old working thread

step 1 When the working thread is down to about 6 in. (15 cm) long, remove the needle. Thread the needle with a new length of thread, ready to join into the beadwork.

step 2 Bring the newly threaded needle up six to eight beads diagonally back from the bead from which the old thread emerges. Thread the needle through the first three or four beads in the direction of the old working thread, leaving a tail of about 6 in. (15 cm).

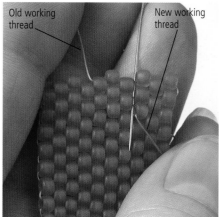

Old working thread

New working thread

step 3 Bring the needle out of the beadwork and then slip it underneath the thread between the nearest pair of beads.

TUBULAR PEYOTE

Tubular peyote creates a hollow tube of beads and can be worked around any cylindrical object, such as a drinking straw, a piece of dowel, or a bottle. Beginners may find it helpful to use a cylinder made of transparent material so that the work can be seen clearly. If you start with an even number of beads, as demonstrated here, you will need to step up at the end of each row in order to move the needle up to the correct position for adding the next row. If using an odd number, you will automatically spiral up to the next row.

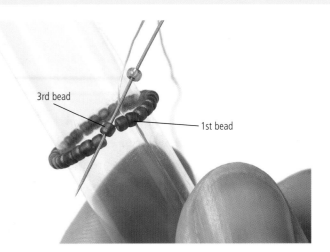

3rd bead

1st bead

step 3 Pick up another bead, then take the needle through the third bead along from the start of the first row. Pull slightly so that the new bead sits neatly on top of the second bead in row 1. Continue in this way until you arrive back at the first bead.

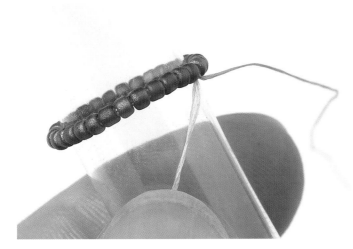

step 1 Thread an even number of beads onto the thread and tie it around a tubular object with a double knot, leaving a tiny gap between the first and last bead in the circle (do not overlap the beads or the stitch will not lie correctly and it will be impossible to work).

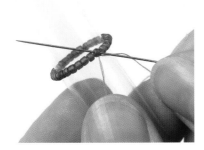

step 2 Thread the needle and take it back through the first bead.

step 4 To step up, take the needle through the first beads of rows 1 and 2 to move up to the next row to be added. Continue adding rows in this way until you reach the required length of the tube.

There are several ways to start and finish off threads, and everyone has their favorite. Some bead workers prefer not to make any knots, instead choosing to weave the ends backward and forward until the thread appears to be secure. Others prefer to tie a discrete knot, feeling that the beadwork seems more secure this way. Try different methods and work with the one that suits you best.

STARTING A THREAD

Always attach a new length of working thread before you finish off the old thread, because it can be difficult to see where the new thread needs to be positioned without the help of the old one.

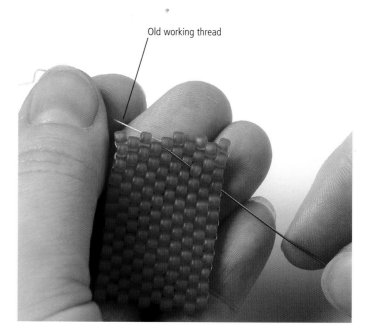

Old working thread

step 2 Bring the newly threaded needle up six to eight beads diagonally back from the bead from which the old thread emerges. Thread the needle through the first three or four beads in the direction of the old working thread, leaving a tail of about 6 in. (15 cm).

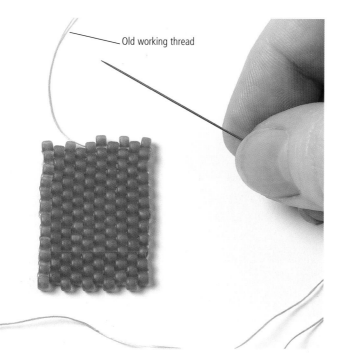

Old working thread

step 1 When the working thread is down to about 6 in. (15 cm) long, remove the needle. Thread the needle with a new length of thread, ready to join into the beadwork.

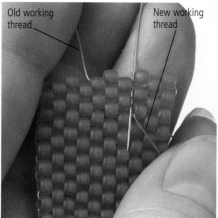

Old working thread

New working thread

step 3 Bring the needle out of the beadwork and then slip it underneath the thread between the nearest pair of beads.

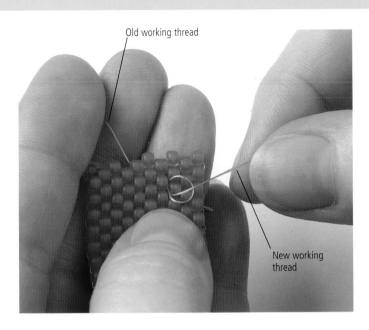

Old working thread

New working thread

step 4 Double knot the new thread by tying one single knot over another.

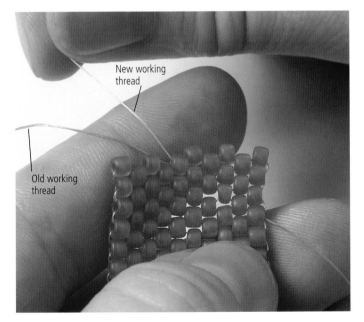

New working thread

Old working thread

step 5 Pass the needle through the next three or four beads, including the bead the old thread is coming out of. Give the thread a slight pull. As you do so, you will either feel or hear a slight click as the knot is pulled inside the next bead, concealing it neatly.

FINISHING A THREAD

When you have joined a new length of working thread, you need to finish off the old one. Any other loose threads, such as the tail end at the start of a piece of beadwork, also need to be tidied up in the same way when the beadwork is complete.

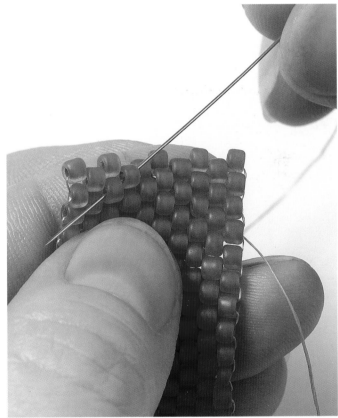

step 6 Rethread the old working thread through the needle. Take the needle through three or four beads in the opposite diagonal direction from the new thread you have just added. Double knot the thread as before, take it through another three or four beads, then click the knot into place. Cut off any excess thread.

Project 1: SEASHORE BRACELET

The base of this bracelet is made from triangle beads using flat even-count peyote stitch. Triangle beads slot together very well and reflect light beautifully. Embellishment, of course, is the key element in this bracelet, providing a great opportunity for you to indulge your creative side.

MAKING THE BASE

step 1 Using eight triangle beads as a starting point, work a length of peyote stitch long enough to fit around the wrist, allowing about ⅝ in. (1.5 cm) for the clasp (see Even-count peyote, page 28).

step 2 When the bracelet foundation is complete, attach the clasp (see Bar clasps, page 100). Finish off the loose ends of thread (see Finishing a thread, page 35).

ADDING THE BASE FRINGE

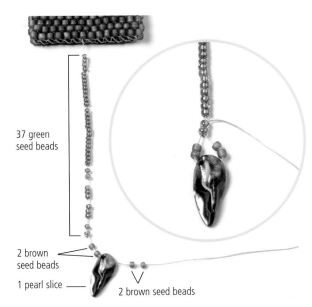

37 green
seed beads

2 brown
seed beads

1 pearl slice

2 brown seed beads

Accent-topped fringe

Small
branch

step 6 At each end of the
base of the purse, work five shorter fringes using brown seed
beads. End each fringe with an amber accent bead topped with
a green seed bead, and add smaller branches using two green
seed beads topped with a brown seed bead.

step 4 Bring the needle out at either of the two central
beads at the base of the purse, ready to work the longest fringe
(see Adding a fringe, page 102). Using size 11 seed beads,
thread on 37 green seed beads, 2 brown seed beads, 1 pearl
slice, and 2 brown seed beads, then thread back up through
the last 2 green seed beads added.

2 beads
between
branches

step 5 Work branch fringing all the way back up the
initial beads, spacing them two green beads apart and using two
green seed beads topped with a brown bead for each branch
(see Branch fringing, page 103). Work two more branch fringes
with a pearl slice at the base on either side of the central fringe,
shortening the length of the fringes as you work outward.

step 7 Extend the fringe up the left side of the purse
by passing the needle through the beads in the actual body
of the purse to the required position for each fringe. Position
five amber-topped brown fringes near the bottom and several
brown-topped green fringes a little further up. Sew a pearl slice
to the center front of the purse.

ATTACHING THE STRAP

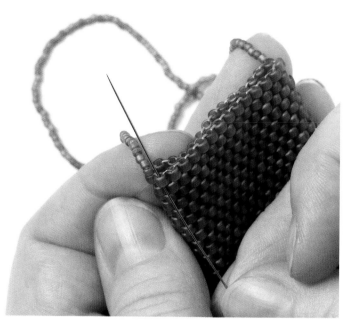

step 8 Thread a beading needle with 5 ft. (1.5 m) of beading thread. Flatten the purse at the top so that there is a pair of seed beads at each side. Bring the needle up through the front seed bead at one side of the purse. Using size 11 brown seed beads, thread on enough beads for the length of the strap required. Take the needle down through the front seed bead on the opposite side of the purse.

step 9 Turn the needle and bring the thread up through the back seed bead of the pair to secure the strap.

10th bead

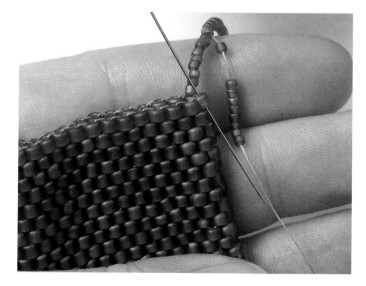

step 10 Thread on nine more brown beads, then pass the needle through the tenth bead up on the original strap. Continue threading the needle through all the beads on the strap until you reach the last 10 beads on the other side of the strap.

step 11 Thread on nine more beads, then pass the needle down through the back seed bead to mirror the other side of the strap.

EMBELLISHING THE STRAP

step 12 Work a small amount of branch fringing into the strap, extending down onto the top right corner of the purse. Add a fringe edging around the top of the purse by coming up through each bead at the edge of the purse, threading on two size 11 green seed beads and one size 11 brown seed bead. Take the needle around the brown bead, through the green beads, and then through the bead on the purse. Bring the needle up through the next bead along the edge of the purse, ready to add the next branch. Finish off any loose ends of thread as before.

USING MATTE BEADS FOR THE PURSE ALLOWS THE IRIDESCENT PEARL SLICES TO STAND OUT. THEY ALSO PROVIDE EFFECTIVE HIGHLIGHTS AT THE ENDS OF THE SHINY-BEAD FRINGING.

Brick stitch is a more solid stitch than many of the other widely used beadwork techniques. If you look at a flat piece of brick stitch, you will see that it resembles a brick wall, hence the name. Brick stitch is often used in its tubular form to create amulet purses, and since it is a fairly firm stitch, it can also be used to create freestanding beadwork, such as vessels and three-dimensional pieces. Brick stitch is best worked with a single strand of thread because the thread passes through each bead twice.

Getting the tension right

To keep the tension firm, pull the working thread back toward you and the tail end of the thread. If you pull the thread away from the beadwork, the tension will slacken and the beads will become too spaced. However, be careful not to pull the thread too strongly or the beadwork will overtighten and become wavy.

MAKING A LADDER

The first stage in working brick stitch is to form a foundation row, known as a ladder. Many amulet purses have a bugle ladder top.

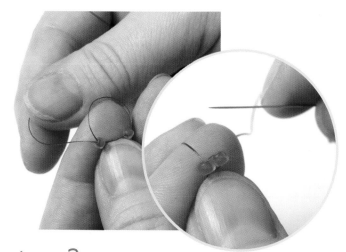

step 2 Pull the ends of the thread in opposite directions so that the beads click together snugly side by side.

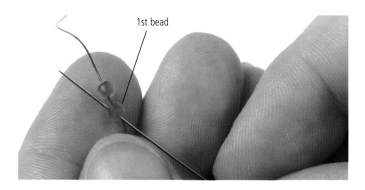

1st bead

step 1 Thread a beading needle with 5 ft. (1.5 m) of beading thread. Thread two beads down to within 6 in. (15 cm) of the tail end of the thread, then bring the needle back through the first bead.

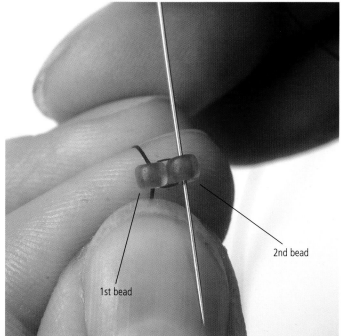

2nd bead

1st bead

step 3 Holding the beads between a thumbnail and forefinger, take the needle back down through the second bead once again.

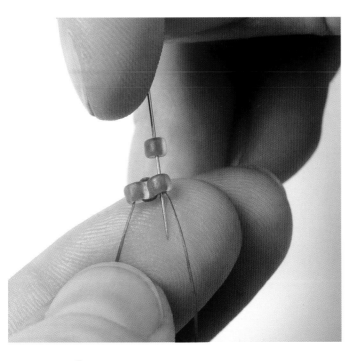

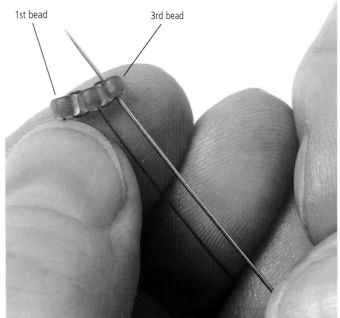

1st bead   3rd bead

step 4 Pick up a bead and take the needle back down through the second bead added. Pull the thread through and down toward the tail end until the third bead sits next to the second bead.

step 5 Thread the needle back up through the third bead so that it is in the correct position to add the next bead.

step 6 Continue adding beads in this way until you reach the required length. Notice that you are alternating between taking the needle through the top and bottom of the previous bead added. Remember not to thread the needle through the hole from which the working thread is emerging.

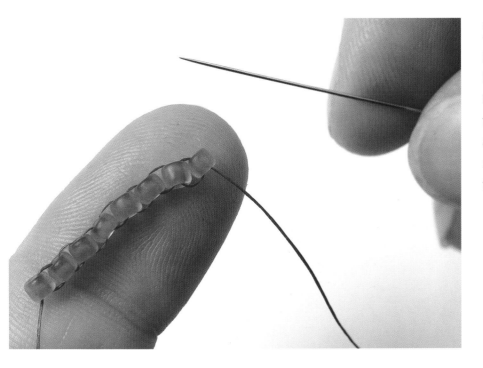

ADDING MORE ROWS

Once the foundation ladder is complete, you can start adding rows of brick stitch.

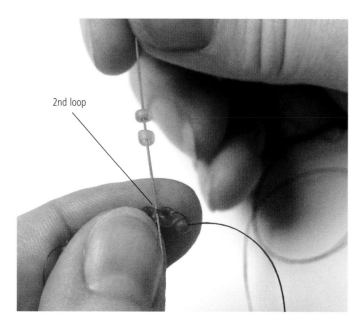

2nd loop

step 7 To start row 2, the thread should be coming out of the top of the last bead added to the ladder. Pick up two beads and take the needle through the second loop of thread along the ladder, from back to front.

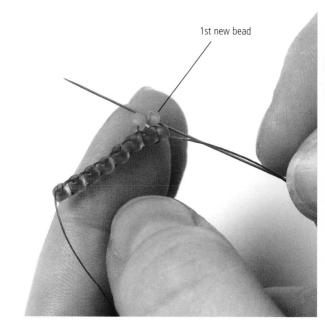

1st new bead

step 8 Allowing the two new beads to sit side by side with the holes facing upward, take the needle back up through the first new bead.

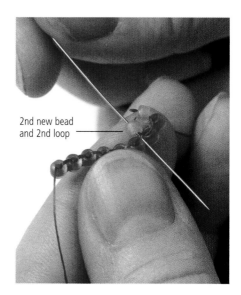

2nd new bead and 2nd loop

step 9

Take the needle back down through the second new bead, then under the loop of the ladder once more.

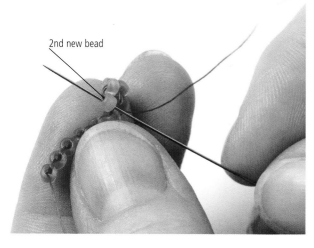

2nd new bead

step 10 Take the needle back up through the second bead again. These moves at the beginning of each row form a locking stitch that will help anchor the first bead and stop it from tipping inward so that you achieve a flat, even piece of beadwork.

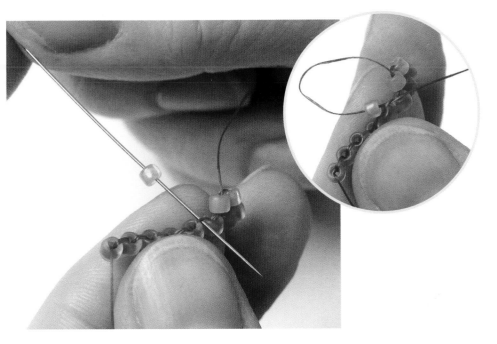

step 11
Pick up a third bead and take the needle under the next loop along on the ladder. Pull the thread through the loop until the new bead sits next to the other two beads added on this row.

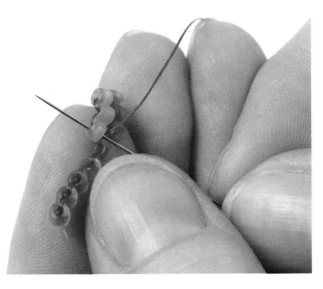

step 12
Thread the needle back up through the third bead, gently pulling upward until all three beads sit in a row. Continue in this way, adding one bead at a time along the row.

step 13
To work row 3, turn the beadwork over so that the working end of the thread is nearest your fingertips. Add two new beads at the beginning of the row as before, threading the needle under the last loop of row 2. Continue adding single beads along the rest of the row. Add subsequent rows in this way until the beadwork reaches the required length.

INCREASING

This technique can be used to increase as many beads as you wish on the outside edge of the beadwork.

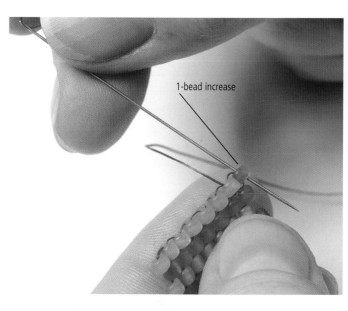

1-bead increase

step 2 Take the needle back down through the bead just added.

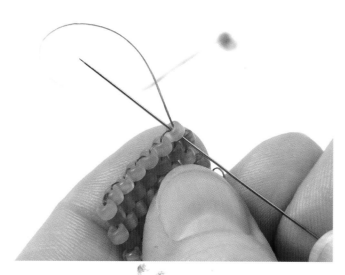

step 1 When you reach a point where you require an increase, thread on one bead, then go back up through the bead from which the thread is emerging.

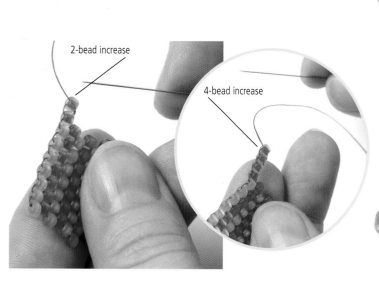

2-bead increase

4-bead increase

step 3 Add another increase bead in the same way. Continue adding beads until you have increased by the required amount.

step 4 Continue to work the next row in brick stitch, working across the increase beads and then the rest of the previous row.

DECREASING

Use this method to decrease beads on the outside edge of the beadwork. In this example, a ladder of seven beads is being decreased symmetrically to a point.

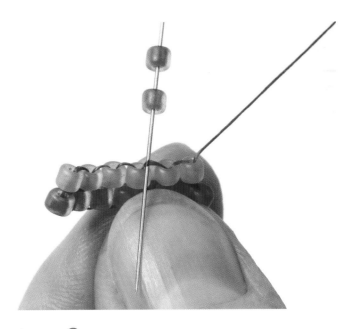

step 1 After working the ladder (see page 42), start row 2 by adding two beads, threading the needle under the second loop in from the end of the ladder (see Adding more rows, page 44). Secure the beads in the usual way, then continue along the row, adding one bead at a time.

step 2 To start row 3, add two beads in the same way as before, threading the needle under the second loop in from the end of row 2. Complete the row, adding one bead at a time.

Row 7 = 1 bead
Row 6 = 2 beads
Row 5 = 3 beads
Row 4 = 4 beads
Row 3 = 5 beads
Row 2 = 6 beads
Row 1 = 7 beads

step 3 As you add more rows, starting each row by threading the needle under the second loop in from the end of the previous row when adding the first pair of beads, the beadwork will decrease down to a point. You could then thread back down through the beadwork to one of the outside beads on the ladder row and repeat this process on the other side to create a diamond shape.

Project 3: VICTORIAN CHOKER

This choker is guaranteed to bring a touch of elegance to any outfit. The neck band of bugle beads is softened by a central fringe that drapes beautifully. The neck band is a great way to familiarize yourself with making the ladder that is used to start brick stitch.

MAKING THE NECK BAND

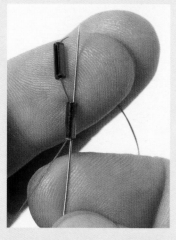

step 1
Thread a beading needle with 1 yd. (1 m) of beading thread. Start the ladder by passing two bugle beads down to within 6 in. (15 cm) of the tail end of the thread. Bring the needle back through the first bead.

step 2
Continue adding bugle beads until you have the required length of ladder, allowing about ⅝ in. (1.5 cm) for the clasp (see Making a ladder, page 42).

ADDING THE FRINGE

1 seed bead

1 bugle bead

3 seed beads

Needle at center point

step 3
Fold the bugle ladder in half to determine where the center is. The fringe consists of 17 strands that increase in length symmetrically toward the center. In this instance, the use of bugle beads dictates the length of the shortest strand, so this strand is added first instead of starting at the center, which is usually recommended (see Adding a fringe, page 102). Count eight bugles out from the center bead, then pass the needle down through that bugle. Thread on one seed bead, one bugle bead, and three seed beads.

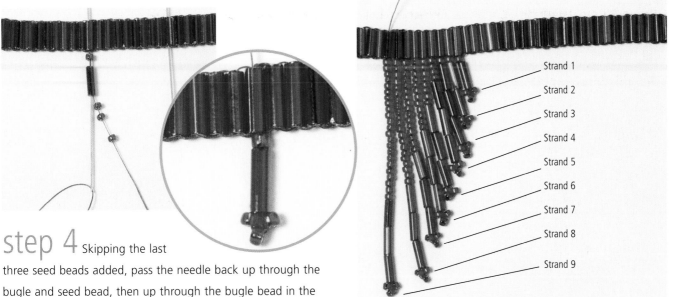

step 4
Skipping the last three seed beads added, pass the needle back up through the bugle and seed bead, then up through the bugle bead in the ladder from which the fringe is emerging. Gently pull the thread so that the seed bead sits snugly against the bugle in the ladder.

Strand 1
Strand 2
Strand 3
Strand 4
Strand 5
Strand 6
Strand 7
Strand 8
Strand 9

1 seed bead

2 bugle beads

3 seed beads

step 5
Pass the needle down through the next bugle toward the center of the ladder. Thread on one seed bead, two bugles, and three seed beads. Skipping the last three seed beads added, pass the needle back up through the remaining beads and then through the ladder bugle from which the fringe is hanging. Take the needle back down through the next bugle toward the center of the ladder.

step 6
Continue to add seven more fringes, adding the following beads:

Strand 3: 1 seed, 3 bugles, 3 seeds.
Strand 4: 4 seeds, 3 bugles, 3 seeds.
Strand 5: 8 seeds, 3 bugles, 3 seeds.
Strand 6: 12 seeds, 3 bugles, 3 seeds.
Strand 7: 16 seeds, 3 bugles, 3 seeds.
Strand 8: 21 seeds, 3 bugles, 3 seeds.
Strand 9: 23 seeds, 3 bugles, 3 seeds.

step 7
When strand 9 is completed at the center of the choker, add another eight strands on the other side, making sure they reduce in length symmetrically to the first side. When the fringe is complete, attach the clasp (see page 98), then finish off the loose ends of thread (see Finishing a thread, page 35).

THIS CHOKER HAS BEEN CREATED ENTIRELY IN BRIGHT RED BEADS FOR A DRAMATIC EFFECT, BUT YOU COULD USE A VARIETY OF BEAD COLORS IN THE DESIGN IF YOU WISH.

Project 4: VICTORIAN EARRINGS

These earrings match the choker featured on the previous pages. They are made up of monocolor bugle and seed beads to give a simple but stylish look, but you could use a variety of color combinations for a different effect. Think also about combining matte with shiny beads.

MAKING THE BASE

step 1 Using 1½ ft. (0.5 m) of beading thread, make a ladder of five bugle beads (see Making a ladder, page 42).

step 2 Add a second row of four bugle beads (see Adding more rows, page 44).

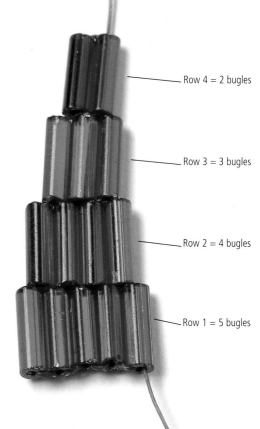

Row 4 = 2 bugles

Row 3 = 3 bugles

Row 2 = 4 bugles

Row 1 = 5 bugles

step 3 Add another two rows in the same way, using three bugles in the third row and two bugles in the fourth (see Decreasing, page 47).

ATTACHING THE FINDING

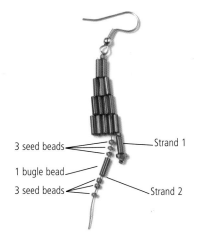

step 4 Thread on one
seed bead, then pass the needle through the loop on one of the
earring findings. Thread the needle back down through the seed
bead, then through the other bugle of the top pair. This makes
the finding sit well between the two bugles. Thread back up and
around the finding again to give added strength.

ADDING THE FRINGE

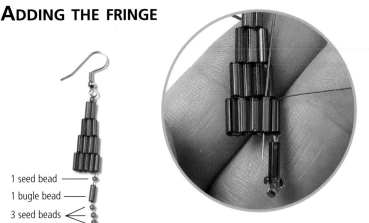

1 seed bead
1 bugle bead
3 seed beads

step 5 When the finding is secure, thread down to
either end of the base bugles, ready to add the fringe (see
Adding a fringe, page 110). Thread on one seed bead, one
bugle, then three seed beads. Skipping the last three seed beads
added, thread back up through the bugle and remaining seed
bead, then back into the bugle on the ladder. Pass the needle
down through the next bugle in the row, ready to add the
second strand.

3 seed beads — Strand 1
1 bugle bead
3 seed beads — Strand 2

step 6 Thread on: three seeds,
one bugle, three seeds. Skipping the last
three seed beads added, thread back up
as before, then down through the third
bugle on the ladder.

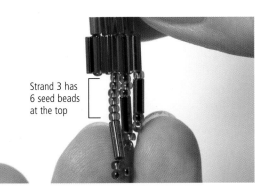

Strand 3 has
6 seed beads
at the top

step 7 Add the central strand, using
six seeds, one bugle, and three seeds. Thread back
up as before, then pass the needle down through
the fourth bugle. Add the fourth strand to match
the second, and the fifth strand to match the first,
so that you have symmetrical fringing at the
bottom of the earring. Finish off any loose ends of
thread (see Finishing a thread, page 35). Make a
matching earring in the same way.

*THE THREE BEADS AT THE ENDS OF
THE FRINGING COULD BE REPLACED
WITH TINY ACCENT BEADS. THESE
WOULD ATTRACT ATTENTION AS
THE FRINGE MOVES WHEN WORN.*

Square stitch beadwork looks similar to loomwork but has the advantage that there are fewer ends of thread to finish off. Square stitch also produces hardwearing pieces because the thread travels through each bead several times, almost creating a fabric of its own. This stitch is excellent for creating patterns because the beads sit in grid formation. Cross-stitch patterns can be worked to stunning effect—just follow them as you would if stitching—or create your own designs using graph paper and colored pencils. Square stitch is best worked with a single strand of thread because the thread passes through each bead several times.

Getting the tension right

It is relatively easy to keep the tension correct with square stitch. Use a stop bead to keep the thread straight on the first two rows. Once you have been through these rows again with the thread to straighten them, the subsequent rows will sit right.

WORKING SQUARE STITCH

Cylinder beads are ideal for square stitch because they are uniform and sit neatly side by side. They also have fairly large holes, making it easier to accommodate the amount of thread that passes through each bead.

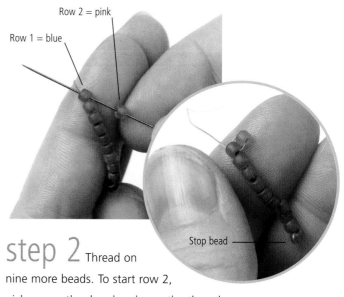

Row 2 = pink
Row 1 = blue
Stop bead

step 2 Thread on nine more beads. To start row 2, pick up another bead and pass the thread back through the last bead on row 1.

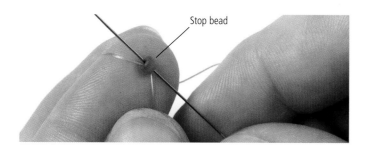

Stop bead

step 1 Thread a beading needle with 5 ft. (1.5 m) of beading thread. Pick up a bead and slide it to within 6 in. (15 cm) of the tail end of the thread. Bring the needle back up through the bead, creating a loop around the bead. This is called a stop bead.

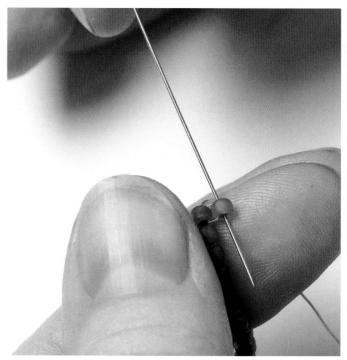

step 3 Take the needle back through the bead just added to start off row 2.

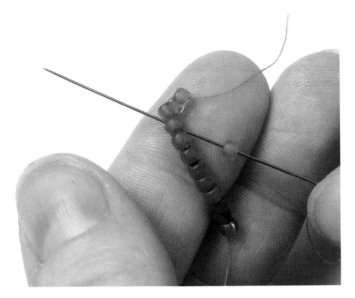

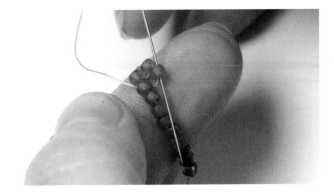

step 5 Thread the needle back through the bead just added on row 2. Continue along the row in this way.

step 4 Pick up another bead and take the needle back through the next to last bead on row 1.

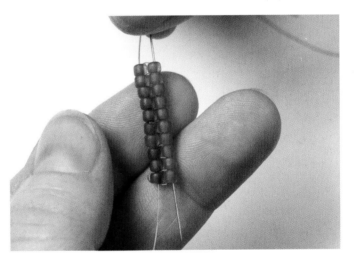

step 7 Turn the needle and take it back through the second row of beads. Pull the thread through so that the two rows sit neatly together. Continue adding rows in this way.

step 6 At this point, the beads may seem to be sitting slightly unevenly. To secure them together, pass the needle back through the first row of beads. Pull the thread through.

BEADER'S TIP

Square stitch involves passing the thread through the beads several times, so it is a good idea to use thread conditioner. There are several types, from synthetic to natural conditioners such as beeswax, that help to prevent the thread from splitting and wearing. If the needle gets stuck, use flat nose pliers to help pull it through, but do not pull too firmly or the bead can shatter.

INCREASING

Shaping techniques allow you to produce intricate shapes, such as butterflies and flowers. This method allows you to increase beads on either of the outside edges of the work.

Increase bead · · · · · ·   1st bead of new row

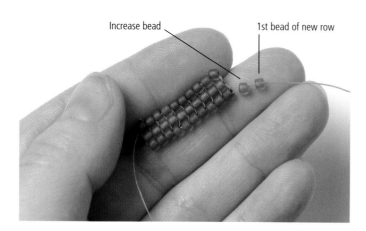

step 1 Bring the needle through the last bead on the row you wish to increase. Thread on one more bead (the increase bead) plus the first bead of the next row.

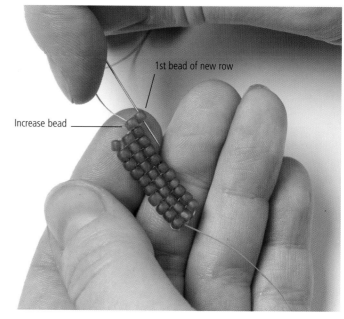

1st bead of new row

Increase bead

step 3 Thread the needle through the first bead of the new row (the last bead added).

1st bead of new row

Increase bead

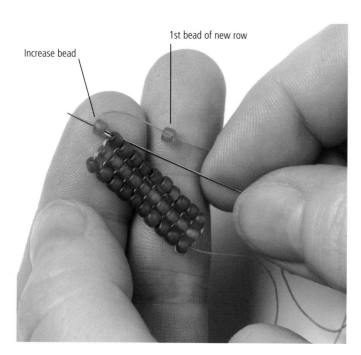

step 2 Skipping the last bead added, thread the needle back through the increase bead.

step 4 Continue working square stitch along the row. Note that you can add as many beads as you wish for an increase, then simply square stitch your way back into the main section of the beadwork to secure.

DECREASING

As with increasing, decreasing is also fairly straightforward in square stitch. This technique allows you to decrease beads on the outside edge of the work.

step 2 Thread on a bead, go back through the bead the thread is coming out of, then back through the bead just added.

step 1 When you finish the row just before the one you need to decrease, thread back as usual through the previous row and then through the row just added. However, instead of taking the needle through to the end of this row, bring it out where you wish the decrease to begin.

step 3 Continue along the row until you reach the bead where you wish to stop the row. Secure the beads in the usual way and continue adding rows of square stitch.

TUBULAR SQUARE STITCH

Tubular square stitch is easier to master when worked around a cylinder, such as a drinking straw, pen, or plastic tube. This technique can be used to create rope necklaces, tubes, and vessels.

step 1 Using a 1-yd. (1-m) length of beading thread, thread on as many beads as necessary to fit around the cylinder.

step 3 Place the circle of beads around the cylinder again. Pull the ends of the thread in opposite directions to tighten the beads firmly together, then tie the thread in a double knot to secure into place.

step 2 Remove the beads from the cylinder and pass the needle through the beads a few at a time from the tail end upward, leaving the beads in a loose circle.

step 4 Thread the needle through the first bead of row 1.

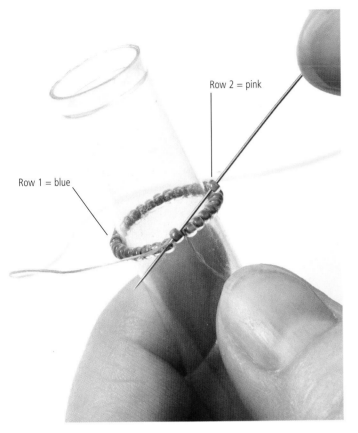

Row 2 = pink

Row 1 = blue

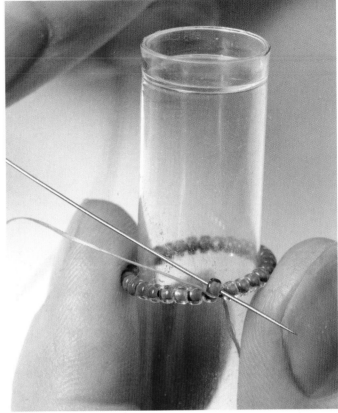

step 5 Pick up the first bead of row 2, then thread the needle through the first bead of row 1 again.

step 6 Thread the needle through the first bead of row 2 again. Notice that you are working counterclockwise. Continue adding beads all around row 2 in this way.

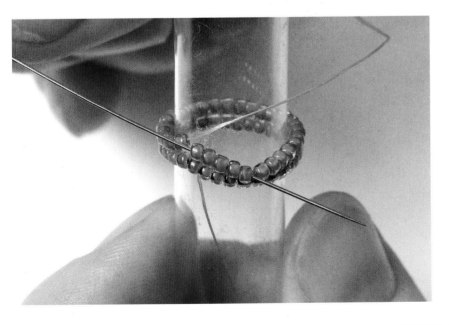

step 7 When the row is complete, take the thread through all the beads on row 2 once more, then bring the needle out through the first bead added on row 2. Add a third row of beads in the same way, but this time work clockwise around the cylinder. Add as many rows as required, working counterclockwise on even-numbered rows and clockwise on odd-numbered rows.

Project 5: RAINBOW BRACELET

This bracelet uses the colors of the rainbow in a zigzag pattern. Refer to the color wheel on page 22 to help select a palette of colors, choosing the primary colors first and then filling in the gaps. Keep trying different tints and shades of each color until you are happy with the overall effect.

MAKING THE BASE

step 1 Starting at the top left corner of the chart on page 59, thread the first 19 seed beads onto a 1-yd. (1-m) length of beading thread to form the first row of the bracelet. Check that the colors are in the same order in which they appear on the chart.

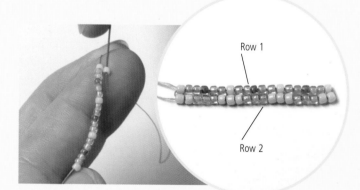

Row 1

Row 2

step 2 Add the second row of beads using square stitch (see page 52), remembering to change color as indicated on the chart. You may find it useful to place a sheet of white paper on the chart just below the row you are working on to avoid confusion.

step 3 Work down the chart, changing colors as required. When you reach the end of the chart, repeat from the top again until the bracelet is long enough to fit around the wrist, allowing about ⅝ in. (1.5 cm) for the fastener.

MAKING THE FASTENER

step 4 Thread 1 yd. (1 m) of thread through an 8 mm bead and tie it with a double knot, leaving a 6-in. (15-cm) tail. Thread on five yellow seed beads, then pass the needle through the 8 mm bead so that the yellow beads loop around the larger bead. Continue adding strings of seed beads until the central bead is fully covered, following a rainbow color order. Make a second embellished bead in the same way. Finish off the loose ends of thread on all the pieces (see Finishing a thread, page 35).

step 5

To add the embellished beads, bring the needle with 1 yd. (1 m) of thread out of the fifth bead on the end row of the bracelet. Thread on one seed bead of any color, then take the thread through one of the embellished beads. Add a second seed bead of the same color as the first one. Skipping this second seed bead, take the needle down through the embellished bead, the first seed bead, and then through the fifth bead on the bracelet again. Repeat this journey two or three times for extra strength. Add the second embellished bead in the same way, five beads from the other edge (see Bead and loop fasteners, page 101).

step 6

To add the loops, bring the needle with 1 yd. (1 m) of thread out through the fifth bead on the opposite end of the bracelet. Thread on 21 seed beads in rainbow color order, then take the needle back down through the first bead added to create a loop. Thread the needle through the fifth bead on the bracelet again, then repeat this journey two or three times for extra strength. Add a second beaded loop in the same way, five beads from the other edge. Finish off any loose ends of thread as before.

BEADER'S TIP

Seed beads are not always exactly the same size, so check that the fastening loop fits over the embellished 8 mm bead before securing the loop to the bracelet. Use more or fewer beads if required to produce a snug fit, remembering that beading thread only gives a small amount.

Start from here, then repeat from this point until bracelet reaches required length

IT IS EASY TO CREATE YOUR OWN UNIQUE BEADING DESIGN USING GRAPH PAPER AND COLORED PENCILS, THEN COLOR MATCH THE BEADS TO THE DRAWING.

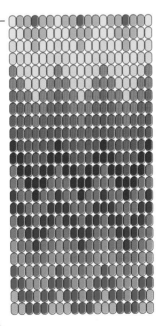

RAINBOW NECKLACE

This necklace can be worn with the strands twisted or gently draped around the neck. One of the main features of the necklace is the end caps, which create a wonderfully neat but decorative finish. As with the matching bracelet on the previous pages, use the color wheel on page 22 to help you select a rainbow color palette.

MAKING THE TUBE

step 1
Thread 24 beads onto 1 yd. (1 m) of beading thread in rainbow color order, leaving a 6-in. (15-cm) tail end. Pass the needle from the tail end upward through the 24 beads once again to form a circle.

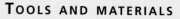

TOOLS AND MATERIALS

- 10 g size 11 seed beads: 12 rainbow colors
- Two gold eyepins
- Two 4-in. (1.5-cm) long gold end caps
- Lobster clasp and jump ring
- Beading thread: ash
- Beading needle
- ⅜ in. (1 cm) cylinder to bead around, such as an empty bead tube
- Beading mat
- Scissors
- Clear nail polish
- Cutting pliers
- Round nose pliers

step 2
Place the circle of beads around the cylinder. Pull the thread tight so that the beads sit firmly together, then tie the thread in a double knot to secure.

BEADER'S TIP

It is a good idea to lay out small piles of beads in the correct color order on a beading mat. This will make beading a little quicker because you will not have to stop and think about which color to add next.

step 3 Work a
second row of tubular
square stitch (see page 56).
You will be working
counterclockwise on this row, so in
order to make the colors swirl around the tube, each new bead
you add on row 2 should be the same color as the bead that sits
to the left of the bead from which the thread emerges. As you
continue around the tube, you will see each pair of beads in the
same color begin to create a diagonal stripe.

step 4 Continue to work tubular square stitch, adding
the colors in the correct order so that they spiral around the
tube. Work 22 rows in total. Finish off the loose ends of thread
(see Finishing a thread, page 35).

MAKING THE STRANDS

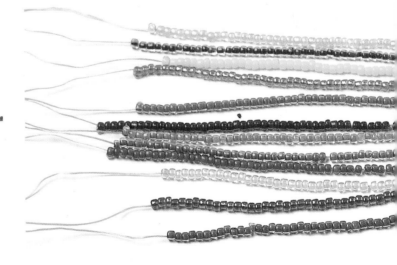

step 5 Decide what length you want the necklace to
be, allowing about ⅝ in. (1.5 cm) for the clasp. If you are going
to twist the strands, allow a little extra length because twisting
will shorten the necklace slightly. Cut 12 pieces of beading
thread to this length, plus 12 in. (30 cm) for finishing. Thread a
seed bead onto the thread, leaving a 6-in. (15-cm) tail end. Pass
the thread through the bead once again to create a stop bead.
Thread on as many beads in the same color as necessary to fill
the thread, leaving another 6-in. (15-cm) tail at the other end.

step 6 Repeat until you have 12 strands of beads, one
in each color of the rainbow.

ATTACHING THE CLASP

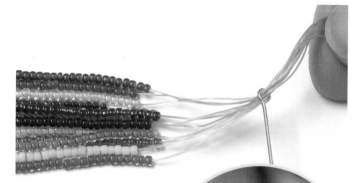

step 9 When the nail polish is thoroughly dry, cut the spare ends of threads as close to the knot as possible.

step 7 Thread the ends of the strands with no stop beads through an eyepin. Tie them onto the eyepin with a knot.

step 8 Tighten the knot as much as possible, then put a small dab of clear nail polish onto it for added strength.

step 10 At the other end of the strands, remove the loops from the stop beads by gently pushing the needle between the loop and stop bead and pulling the thread through. When they are all free, hold up all 12 ends vertically to see if you need to remove any beads from this end to make all the beading even. Attach this end to an eyepin as before.

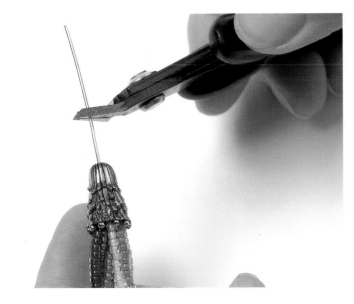

step 11 Thread an end cap onto one of the eye pins so that it covers all the messy ends of thread. Using cutting pliers, cut off the wire end just under halfway down.

step 12 Place a pair of round nose pliers directly above the end cap, then angle the wire toward you at 45 degrees. Move the pliers up toward the top of the wire and bend it around to form an open loop. If the wire is too long for the loop, cut off another small section.

TWIST THE NECKLACE WHEN WEARING IT SO THAT THE STRANDS SWIRL AROUND TO MATCH THE PATTERN ON THE CENTRAL TUBE, OR LEAVE THEM STRAIGHT FOR CONTRAST.

step 13 Slip a lobster clasp onto the loop and squeeze the loop closed with the pliers. Add a jump ring to the other end of the necklace in the same way. Slide the tube onto the center of the strands.

Technique: NETTING STITCH

Netting stitch produces open, lacy beadwork that drapes beautifully around the neck and wrist, but it can also be worked firmly enough to make a tube. The stitch is of slightly more limited use than other techniques, but it is still very effective. The thread pattern of netting stitch is quite involved and delicate, so it is almost always worked with one strand of thread. Using two strands could cause unnecessary knotting and make the overall netting a little too taut, losing much of the stitch's wonderful movement. However, use two strands to create a firmer base for freestanding and three-dimensional beadwork.

Getting the tension right

You may find it best to work this stitch flat on a bead mat so that you can see when the tension needs altering. If the tension is too loose, the thread will show; if it is too tight, the netting will buckle. Try not to pierce the working thread that is already sitting in the bead or there is a strong risk of the beadwork twisting on itself.

FIVE-BEAD NETTING

This forms the basis of all netting stitches, with just the number of beads varying. Two colors of beads are used here for clarity—turquoise (T) and pale green (G).

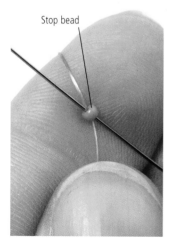

Stop bead

step 1 Thread a beading needle with 1 yd. (1 m) of beading thread and pick up 1T bead. Slide the bead down to within 6 in. (15 cm) of the tail end, then bring the needle back up through the bead to create a stop bead.

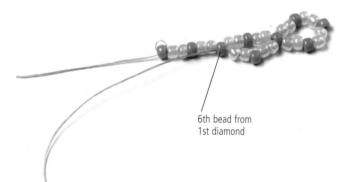

Stop bead

12th bead from working end of thread

step 2 Pick up 2G, 1T beads. Repeat until you have threaded 24 beads in total, including the stop bead. Bring the needle back up through the 12th (turquoise) bead from the working end of the thread. Pull up to form the first diamond, with a turquoise bead at all four points of the diamond.

6th bead from 1st diamond

step 3 Thread 2G, 1T, 2G beads onto the needle. Bring the needle back up through the sixth (turquoise) bead along the first row, counting from the first diamond.

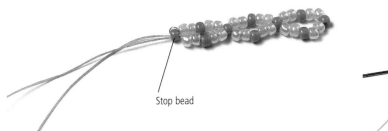

Stop bead

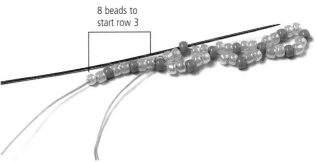

8 beads to start row 3

step 4 Make another diamond in the same way, finishing the row by taking the needle up through the stop bead.

step 5 Pick up 2G, 1T, 2G, 1T, 2G beads. Take the needle down through the middle turquoise bead of the last diamond on the previous row.

step 6 Pick up 2G, 1T, 2G beads. Take the needle down through the middle turquoise bead of the next diamond on the previous row, forming another diamond. Repeat to make a third diamond.

step 7 Pick up 2G, 1T, 2G, 1T, 2G beads. Thread the needle back up through the middle turquoise bead of the remaining diamond on the previous row. Continue adding rows in this way until the netting is the required length.

TUBULAR NETTING

This technique produces a tube of netting that makes effective necklaces and bracelets. Working one netted tube over another also produces an interesting effect. Work this stitch around a cylinder, such as a drinking straw, to help you keep the tension constant. Two colors of beads are used here for clarity— turquoise (T) and pale green (G).

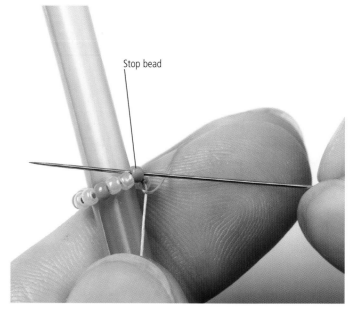

Stop bead

step 3 Take the needle through the first turquoise bead (the stop bead) once again.

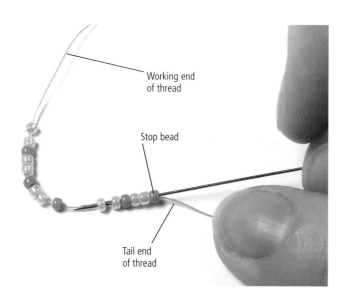

Working end of thread

Stop bead

Tail end of thread

step 1 Thread the needle with beads in the same way as for five-bead netting (see page 64), but thread only 15 beads in total. Pass the needle through all the beads once again, starting at the tail end.

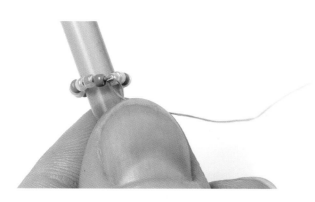

step 2 Place the circle of beads around a cylinder and tie the thread in a double knot.

BEADER'S TIP

When changing thread, take care not to knot the threads too tightly or it will cause a dent in the tube that is impossible to get out. If possible, attach the new thread by threading up through the netting as near as possible to where you need to continue, make a double knot between two beads, then thread through to the required place. When you have worked about another ¾ in. (2 cm) of the stitch, thread the old thread back up and finish in the usual way (see Finishing a thread, page 35).

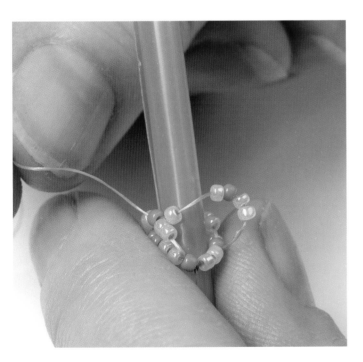

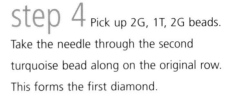

step 4

Pick up 2G, 1T, 2G beads. Take the needle through the second turquoise bead along on the original row. This forms the first diamond.

step 5

Add a second loop in the same way, then pick up 2G, 1T, 2G beads for the third loop. There will only be one turquoise bead left on the first row (the bead at the start of the row). To attach the third loop, you need to go through the turquoise bead in the middle of the first diamond you added.

step 6

Pick up 2G, 1T, 2G beads. Take the needle through the turquoise bead in the middle of the second diamond you added. This forms the first diamond of the new row. Note how the tube is spiraling upward. Continue adding diamonds until the tube is the required length.

Project 7: SUMMER AMULET PURSE

A netted section of beadwork is reminiscent of a garden trellis. Intertwined with vines and flowers, it makes the perfect summer purse. The base is a net of seed beads with a ladder stitch bugle bead top, finished with a single string of beads as a strap. The surface embellishment of seed beads and flower accent beads transform the simple base into a delightful amulet purse.

TOOLS AND MATERIALS

- 10 g 6 mm bugle beads: dark green
- 10 g size 11 seed beads: pale green
- 10 g size 11 seed beads: turquoise
- Bellflower accent beads: pastel colors
- Beading thread: ash
- Beading needle
- Beading mat
- Scissors

MAKING THE PURSE BASE

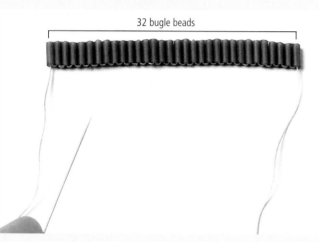

32 bugle beads

step 1
Thread a beading needle with 5 ft. (1.5 m) of beading thread. Make a ladder of 32 bugle beads (see Making a ladder, page 42). Flip the ladder over so that the working thread is coming down through the first bugle on the left side.

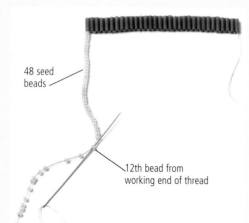

48 seed beads

12th bead from working end of thread

step 2
Thread on 48 pale green seed beads. Pass the needle up through the 12th bead along from the working end of the thread, pulling up the thread gently to form the first diamond (see Five-bead netting, page 64).

6th bead along

5 beads

step 3
Thread on five more pale green seed beads. Skipping the next five beads on the initial row, pass the needle through the sixth bead to form the second diamond.

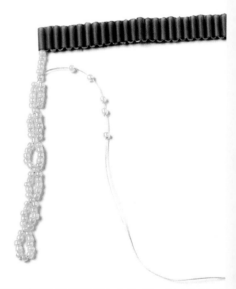

step 4
Continue adding sets of five beads and then threading through the sixth bead on the initial row until you reach the bugle ladder.

2nd bugle

3rd bugle

step 5
Pass the needle through the top
seed bead on the initial row, then take the needle through
the next bugle. You will see that the first row of netting sits
neatly beneath the first and second bugles on the ladder.
Take the needle down through the third bugle.

8 beads

step 7
When you reach the
bottom of the row, you need to add
eight beads. This will allow you to turn
the needle in order to work the stitch
back up the netting.

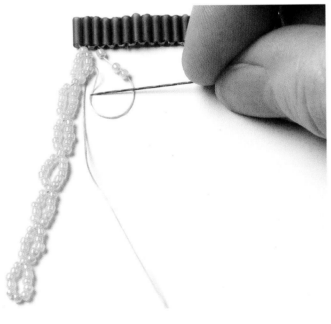

step 6
To work the next row of netting, you only
need to add three pale green seed beads to complete the first
half diamond at the top of the row. Complete the remaining
diamonds by adding five beads each time, threading through
each central bead of the five added on the previous row.

5 beads

step 8
Continue adding
rows of netting stitch until you reach
the next to last bugle. Work the next row of
netting down the purse as before, but when you work the
bottom diamond, use five beads instead of the usual eight. Bring
the needle through the central bead of the bottom diamond on
the other side of the purse, joining the two sides together.

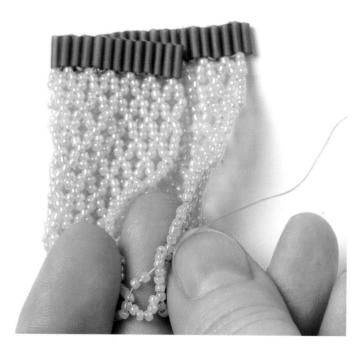

step 10 Make sure that the points at the base of the purse match front and back. When you are happy with the alignment, join the central beads at each pair of diamond points using square stitch (see page 52). Finish off the loose ends of thread (see Finishing a thread, page 35).

step 9 Take a good look at the bead pattern to figure out where the two side edges need to be joined in order to maintain the netting pattern. Join the edges, adding two beads and then running the needle through the central beads of the diamonds on alternate edges to complete the pattern.

EMBELLISHING THE PURSE

step 11 Thread the needle down through the bugle at the top right side of the purse. Add a piece of branch fringing diagonally across the front of the purse from top right to bottom left using turquoise seed beads (see Branch fringing, page 102). Weave the fringe in and out of the netting at regular intervals to hold it in place.

step 12 Add side branches of three, four, or five turquoise beads at intervals. Finish each side branch with a flower accent bead topped with a turquoise seed bead. Note that the fringing extends beyond the bottom edge of the purse. Add a couple more branch fringes extending diagonally outward from the main fringe.

ADDING THE STRAP

step 15
Embellish the right side of the strap with the same style of fringing as on the body of the purse. Finish off any loose ends of thread as before.

step 13
Flatten the purse at the top so that there is a pair of bugles at each side. Bring the needle up through the front bugle at one side of the purse. Thread on pale green seed beads until you reach the required length of strap. Pass the needle down through the front bugle on the opposite side of the purse.

21st bead

step 14
Take the needle up through the back bugle of the pair. Thread on 20 pale green seed beads, then pass the needle through the 21st bead up on the strap. Continue threading the needle through the beads of the strap until you reach 20 beads from the other end. Thread another 20 seed beads onto the needle, then take the needle down through the back bugle to mirror the other side of the strap.

THE BRANCH OF FLOWERS HAS BEEN WORKED IN TURQUOISE TO STAND OUT FROM THE PALE NETTING TRELLIS BUT WITHOUT BEING TOO DOMINANT.

Project 8: GARDEN LARIAT

A lariat is one continual piece of beadwork. It can be hung around the neck and casually knotted or doubled like a scarf with the flower ends pulled through the loop. Worked in two toning colors of seed beads, the bellflower accent beads at each end have the flower heads pointing upward instead of the more usual downward.

TOOLS AND MATERIALS

- 20 g size 11 seed beads: green
- 20 g size 11 seed beads: turquoise
- 16 bellflower accent beads: green
- Beading thread: ash
- Beading needle
- ¼ in. (6 mm) cylinder to bead around, such as a drinking straw
- Beading mat
- Scissors

MAKING THE TUBE

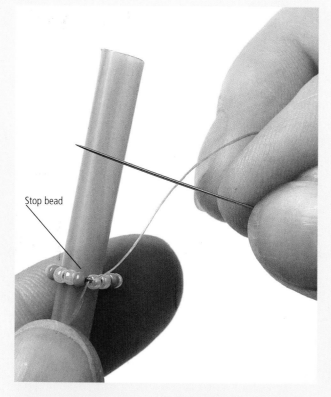

Stop bead

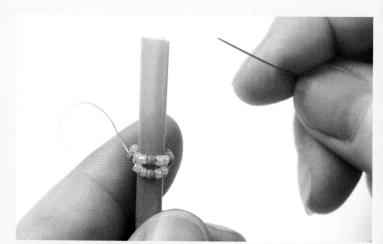

step 2 Pass the needle through the first turquoise seed bead once again, then pick up two green, one turquoise, and two green beads. Skipping the next turquoise bead, pass the needle through the second turquoise bead.

step 1 Work a length of tubular netting in the usual way (see page 66), alternating 1 turquoise seed bead and then 2 green seed beads until you have 15 beads in total. Pass the needle through all 15 beads once again from the tail end upward to form a circle. Place the bead circle over a cylinder and work a double knot between the first and last beads of the circle.

step 3
Continue adding loops of spiraling netting stitch until the tube is the desired length.

step 4
Thread the needle through the turquoise beads at the end of the tube, pull up into a circle, then tie a double knot to secure. Do not finish off the ends of thread.

EMBELLISHING THE TUBE

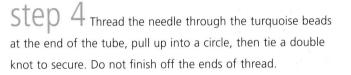

3 seed beads between pairs of accent beads

step 6
Repeat until you have added eight flowers and groups of seed beads in total. Skipping the last three seed beads added, pass the needle back through all the beads and into the netted tube. Repeat at the other end of the tube. Finish off the loose ends of thread (see Finishing a thread, page 35).

step 5
Thread on one bellflower accent bead, then one green, one turquoise, and one green seed bead, followed by another bellflower.

THE TURQUOISE SEED BEADS PROVIDE SUBTLE HIGHLIGHTS IN THE TUBULAR NETTING AND ARE ECHOED IN THE COLORS OF THE ACCENT BEADS.

Technique: SQUARE NETTING STITCH

This version of netting stitch (see page 64) uses four sets of three beads to form square shapes instead of diamonds, giving lots of scope for embellishment. Size 8 seed beads have been used here to demonstrate how to work the stitch, but when you are more confident, you might like to try using size 11 beads—they create a great effect.

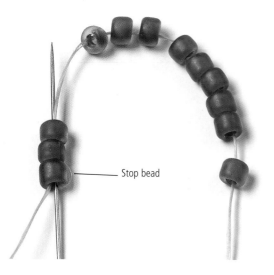

Stop bead

step 2 Thread on another 11 beads, then take the needle through the first set of three beads once more.

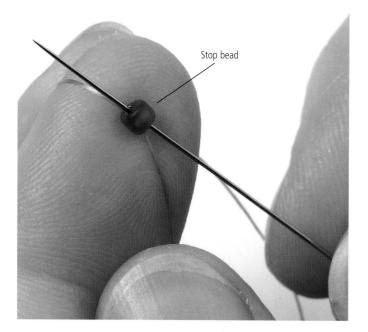

Stop bead

step 1 Thread a beading needle with 1 yd. (1 m) of beading thread and pick up one bead. Slide the bead down to within 6 in. (15 cm) of the tail end of the thread, then bring the needle back up through the bead to create a stop bead.

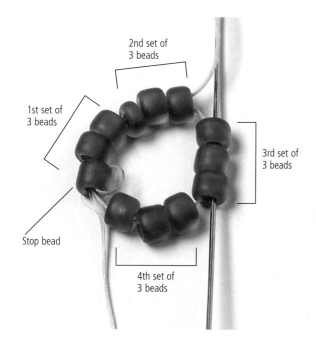

2nd set of 3 beads

1st set of 3 beads

3rd set of 3 beads

Stop bead

4th set of 3 beads

step 3 Thread the needle through the next six seed beads, three beads at a time to keep the square shape of the beadwork. This forms the first square of the net.

BEADER'S TIP

It is important that you always thread the needle through the beads in sets of three beads at a time. This helps to form the square-shaped netting. If you thread through them in one go, you will be encouraging them into a circle shape.

---

step 4
Thread on nine new beads. You do not need 12 beads this time because the first wall of the second square is formed by three beads of the first square. Take the needle back down through the third set of three beads of the first square.

step 5
Thread the needle through the next two sets of three beads of the second square. This brings the needle into the correct position for adding a third square. Continue adding squares until the beadwork reaches the desired length.

step 6
To add a new row of squares, thread on nine more beads. Take the needle back through the three beads of the previous square from which the working thread is trailing.

step 7
Thread back through all the beads just added, three at a time. Take the needle through the bottom three beads of the next square along on the original row, so that the needle is in the correct position to add another square. Continue adding new squares and rows in this way until the desired size is achieved.

Project 9: CRYSTAL BRACELET

This is a great little design for showing off some lovely crystal beads, but you could choose another style of accent bead of a similar size if you prefer. The cleverly disguised fastening formed from a beaded loop and fringe adds a simple but effective decorative touch.

TOOLS AND MATERIALS

- Fifty 6 mm crystal beads: lilac
- 10 g size 11 seed beads: purple
- Beading thread: ash
- Beading needle
- Beading mat
- Scissors

MAKING THE NETTING

step 1 Thread 14 seed beads and one crystal onto 1 yd. (1 m) of beading thread, leaving a 6-in. (15-cm) tail end. Pass the needle from the tail end upward through all the beads once again, then tie a double knot between the crystal and adjacent seed bead. This forms the loop for fastening the bracelet.

step 2 Take the needle back through the crystal, then thread on three sets of three seed beads and one crystal. Thread the needle back through the original crystal to form the first square. This is the same as the square netting stitch described on page 74, but there is a crystal along each side of the square in addition to three seed beads. Take the needle back through the first set of three seed beads and one crystal, then through the next set of three seed beads and one crystal.

step 3 Thread on three seed beads, one crystal, and three more seed beads. Thread the needle back through the crystal from which the working thread is emerging in the first square. You have now formed the small link that appears between each pair of crystal squares of the bracelet. Take the needle through the first three seed beads and crystal that you just added, so that the needle is in the correct position to add another square.

Fastening loop   Small link

Crystal square

step 4 Continue adding crystal squares and small links in this way until the required length is achieved. The tassel fastening can be attached to either a crystal square or a small link, so there is no need to worry about whether the correct length is reached at a square or link.

ADDING THE FRINGE

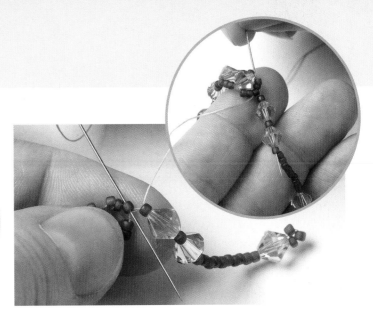

step 5
With the needle coming out of the last crystal, thread on five seed beads. Then pass the needle back through the crystal and the first three of the five seed beads.

1st group of 10 seed beads, where branches will be added later

step 6
Thread on: 1 seed bead, 1 crystal, 1 seed bead, 1 crystal, 10 seed beads, 1 crystal, 3 seed beads. Skipping the last three seed beads, thread the needle back through all the remaining beads just added to form the central fringe (see Adding a fringe, page 102).

step 7
Thread the needle through the middle of the five beads added in step 5. This ensures that the fringe sits centrally on the main netting. Take the needle through the step 5 seed beads and crystal, until it emerges from the middle of the five seed beads once again. Thread down through the central fringe until you are coming out of the first of the group of 10 seed beads added in step 6.

step 8
Thread on eight seed beads to form a second fringe. Skipping the last three beads, pass the needle back up and around as before, until it emerges from the first of the 10 seed beads again, ready to add a third fringe. Make the third fringe using 10 seed beads. Finish off the loose ends of thread (see Finishing a thread, page 35).

PRETTY PURPLE AND LILAC BEADS MAKE THE PERFECT BRACELET FOR A SUMMER OUTFIT, OR YOU COULD TRY BLACK AND GOLD FOR A FORMAL EVENING LOOK.

Project 10: BLUEBELL CHOKER

Czech pressed-glass flower beads in a bluebell design have been used to make this bright and summery choker, but you could easily create an autumnal look by using black or brown cord with accent beads in a leaf design. Rattail cord is comfortable to wear and gives an unusual finish.

TOOLS AND MATERIALS

- 10 g size 11 seed beads: lilac
- 5 g size 11 seed beads: blue
- 5 g 4 mm cube beads: lilac
- 5 bluebell accent beads: blue
- 1 yd. (1 m) rattail cord: blue
- 2 flat leather crimps
- 2 jump rings
- 1 lobster clasp
- Beading thread: ash
- Beading needle
- Beading mat
- Scissors
- Flat nose pliers
- Round nose pliers

MAKING THE NETTING

step 1 Using lilac seed beads, work a single line of 29 squares of square netting stitch (see page 74). When finished, tie a double knot between two beads on the last square to hold the beads in place. Do not finish off the ends of thread because these will be used to secure the beadwork to the cord. Fold the line of squares in half to determine where the middle is.

ADDING THE FRINGE

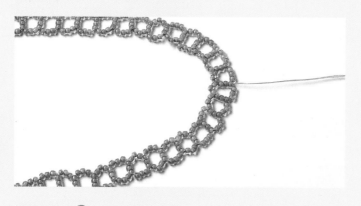

step 2 Join a new thread to the middle of the netting (see Starting a thread, page 34), then thread the needle down through the central row of three vertical lilac beads.

3 sets of 1 blue seed bead and 1 cube bead

1 blue seed bead

1 bluebell

1 blue seed bead

step 3 Add a central fringe (see page 102) by threading on three sets of one blue seed bead and one cube bead. Add another blue seed bead, a bluebell, and one more blue seed bead. Skipping the last seed bead added, thread back up through the fringe, the three vertical lilac beads of the netting, then around and down through the next three vertical lilac beads of the netting.

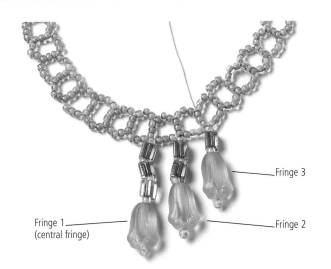

Fringe 3

Fringe 1
(central fringe)

Fringe 2

step 4

Add a second fringe in the same way, but with one less seed bead and cube bead at the beginning. Add a third fringe, again using one less seed bead and cube bead at the beginning. Add another two fringes on the other side of the central fringe, staggering the length of the fringes symmetrically. You can either thread through the beads to the other side or join a fresh piece of thread. Finish off the loose ends of thread on the fringing only (see Finishing a thread, page 35).

ATTACHING THE CORD AND FASTENER

step 5

Cut a length of rattail cord long enough to fit around the neck, adding about 2 in. (5 cm) at each end for adjustments. Carefully thread the cord in and out of the beadwork squares. Move the beadwork to the center of the cord with the fringe hanging down.

step 6

When you are happy with the position, use the threads at each end of the netting to put a couple of securing stitches through the cord. Take the needle through the last three vertical lilac beads of the square netting, then finish off the loose ends of thread as before.

step 7

Hold the choker up against the neck to check that you are happy with the length. Trim the cord symmetrically if necessary. Attach a flat leather crimp and jump ring to each end of the cord, then attach the lobster clasp to one of the jump rings (see page 119).

CHOOSE YOUR ACCENT BEADS FIRST, THEN COMPLEMENT THEM WITH SEED BEADS AND RATTAIL CORD IN APPROPRIATE COLORS.

Project 11: BLUEBELL CHARM BRACELET

This is a charm bracelet with a twist. Instead of having traditional charms, pretty Czech pressed-glass flower beads in bluebell and bellflower designs have been used to complement the choker on page 78. These beads give the bracelet a delicate look, but it could be quite dramatic if worked in black and gold for evening wear.

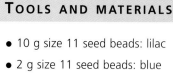
MAKING THE BEADED BASE

step 1
Using lilac seed beads, work a single row of square netting stitch (see page 74) to fit around the wrist, allowing about ⅝ in. (1.5 cm) for the clasp. The design works best if there is an even number of squares because the cube beads are added to the netting in pairs.

step 2
Add a lilac cube bead inside the first square using a cross stitch. Start by bringing the thread out at the top right corner of the last square worked. Thread on a lilac cube bead, then hold the thread diagonally across to the lower left corner of the netted square.

step 3
Take the needle up through the three vertical seed beads on the left side of the square, then thread the needle back down through the lilac cube bead.

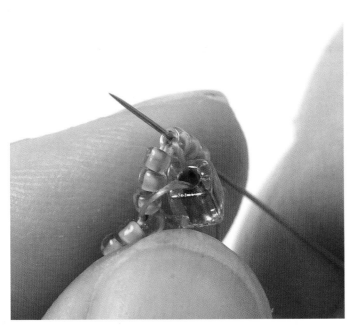

2 lilac seed beads
1 bellflower
1 lilac seed bead

step 4
Pass the needle up through the three vertical seed beads on the right side of the netted square. This will straighten the cube within the square, and you will be able to see the cross stitch formed through the cube. Continue adding cube beads in this way, alternating two lilac beads and two blue beads. You will not always be starting from the same position on the squares, but this is not important as long as a cross stitch is formed through each cube.

step 5
If you are feeling confident, you can add the fringes of accent beads as you apply the cubes; otherwise, add them at the end. Add each fringe by threading down through the three vertical seed beads on the main netting (see page 102). Position an amethyst bellflower between each pair of lilac cube beads, adding two lilac seed beads, then the bellflower and another lilac seed bead for each one. Remember to skip the last seed bead when threading back up through the fringe into the main netting of the bracelet.

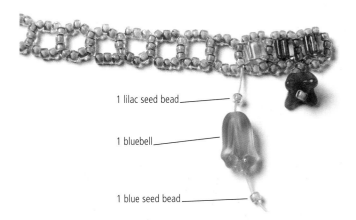

1 lilac seed bead
1 bluebell
1 blue seed bead

THE DIFFERENT LENGTHS OF THE ACCENT BEADS CREATE A STAGGERED LOWER EDGE ON THE BRACELET, ENHANCING THE FEELING OF MOVEMENT IN THE BEADWORK.

step 6
Add the bluebell fringes between each pair of blue cube beads by threading on one lilac seed bead, one bluebell, and then one blue seed bead. Skipping the blue seed bead, thread back up through the fringe and into the netting as before. Finish off the loose ends of thread (see Finishing a thread, page 35) and attach a clasp (see page 98).

Loomwork has a long-established history, dating back to the first Native Americans and many African nations. The technique is still very much alive today, and as well as being popular with adults, loomwork is a great way to introduce children to beadwork. When you look at a section of loomwork and square stitch (see page 52), it is difficult to tell which is which because the thread pattern is similar. Square stitch does not grow as fast as loomwork, but with loomwork you have the time-consuming task of weaving in the loose ends of thread to secure them.

Creating a design

You can either design freehand directly onto the loom as you bead, or prepare a design on graph paper using colored pencils. Cross-stitch embroidery patterns are great for translating into a loomed piece of beadwork because they are also designed on a grid system.

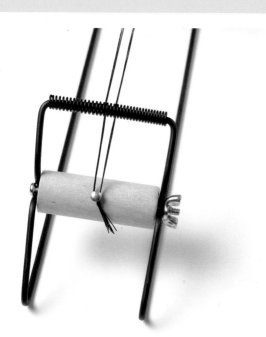

step 2 Turn the spools at each end of the loom so that the pegs face outward from the loom. Place the knots around the pegs with the threads separated into two halves. If you are weaving a piece that is longer than your loom, wind the extra length of threads around the spool farthest away from you.

THREADING A LOOM

Decide on your bead design. If you are working freehand, you need to decide how many beads wide the design will be so that you can set up the loom accordingly. Use a strong synthetic thread for loomwork.

step 1 Cut one more warp (lengthwise) thread than the number of beads wide that the design will be. This design is 9 beads wide, so 10 pieces of thread are required. Cut the thread to the required length, adding an extra 6 in. (15 cm) at each end for finishing off the threads. Knot the threads together at both ends using a double knot.

step 3 Tighten both spools until the threads becomes taut over the separator bars. Use a beading needle to lift the threads into separate adjacent grooves on the separator bars. You may need to loosen the threads a little by adjusting the spools while doing this, but remember to tighten them again afterward.

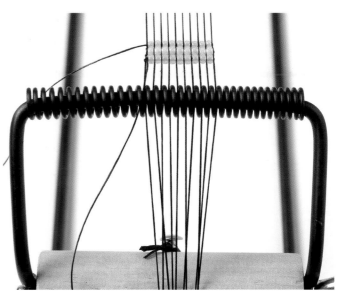

step 4
Once the 10 warp threads are positioned, you need to attach the first weft (crosswise) thread in preparation for adding the beads. Thread a beading needle with 1 yd. (1 m) of beading thread. Tie one end of the thread around the first warp thread in a double knot, leaving a 6-in. (15-cm) tail end.

step 6
Continue adding rows of beads in this way, changing color and building the design as you go. If you are following a chart, check carefully that you are adding the right color beads in the correct order to complete the design.

WEAVING THE BEADS

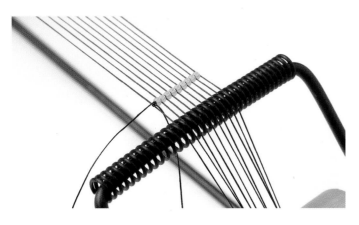

step 5
Thread the first row of beads onto the needle (in this case, nine beads). Position the beads under the loom, pressing them up between the warp threads. Pass the needle and weaving thread through all nine beads, making sure that the needle glides under the warp threads. Holding the beads in place with your finger, bring the needle back through the beads, but this time make sure that it travels over the top of the warp threads. This completes the first row.

FINISHING OFF
- Whenever you finish a length of weaving thread, simply knot a new length of thread onto the outermost warp thread. Remember to leave a tail of thread to allow you to weave in the ends neatly when you have finished beading. When the beadwork has reached the required length, loosen the spools at both ends of the loom and lift the work off.
- Finish off the weft threads by weaving each thread through one or two rows of beads. You can place a double knot between any two beads as you would normally do when finishing off a thread (see page 35), but you need to be very neat or the knot will show and spoil the fabric-like effect that loomwork produces.
- To finish off the warp threads, cut off the knots that you used to secure the threads to the loom; in this demonstration, there would be 10 loose warp threads at each end of the work. Depending on the fastening method you have chosen for the finished item, you may need to work some or all of the warp threads, one at a time, back into the loomwork.

Project 12: FRIENDSHIP BRACELET

This project is a great way to discover loomwork. It is worked from a graph, with pretty little flower motifs set into a pearlized background. The ends are shaped into a point to give a delicate finish. They are worked in square stitch, but as loomwork and square stitch are so similar, the join is almost impossible to see.

MAKING THE BASE

step 1 Thread the loom with 10 strands of beading thread, then add the first weft thread (see Threading a loom, page 82).

step 2 Starting at the top left corner of the chart (see page 85), thread the first nine cream seed beads onto the weaving thread to form the first row of the bracelet. Push the beads up through the warp threads with your finger and pull the needle through the beads beneath the warp threads (see Weaving the beads, page 83).

step 3 Carefully pass the needle back through all the seed beads, making sure you carry the weaving thread over the warp threads this time.

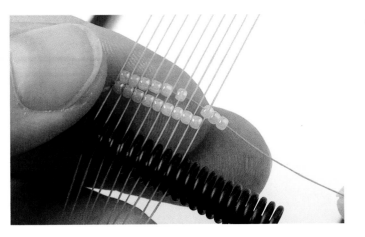

step 4
Thread on all the beads required for the second row and weave them onto the loom as before. Continue in this way, checking carefully that you are following the correct color sequence on the chart. Calculate the length of loomwork required, allowing for four rows of square stitch to be added at each end, plus about ⅝ in. (1.5 cm) for the clasp. Work the chart design until the required length is achieved, finishing with two rows of cream seed beads to match the first end of the bracelet.

SHAPING THE ENDS

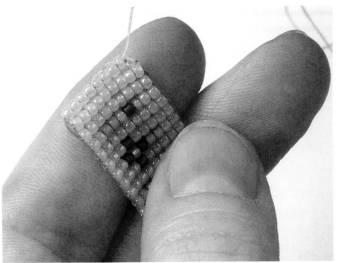

step 5
On the final loomwork row, take the weaving thread back through the final row of beads in the usual way, but bring the needle out of the next to last bead. Remove the beading from the loom.

BEADER'S TIP
This type of loom will only accommodate about 6 in. (15 cm) of beading comfortably, so adding the square stitch ends achieves two things. First, it gives a neat finish; and second, if you need to lengthen the bracelet, you can add several more rows of square stitch the same width as the loomwork section of the bracelet before reducing down to a point. Remember to allow about ⅝ in. (1.5 cm) for the clasp.

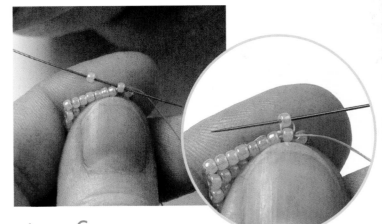

step 6
Pick up a cream bead and pass the needle back through the next to last bead on the final loomwork row. Turn the needle and take it back through the bead just added.

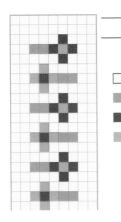

—— Start from here

—— Repeat from here until bracelet reaches correct length

☐ cream

▨ green

■ purple

▨ pink

FRIENDSHIP BRACELET**85**

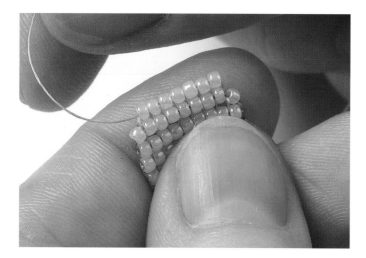

step 7
Continue working square stitch (see Working square stitch, page 52) until you reach the last bead on the opposite side of the bracelet. Do not add a bead at this end so that the width of the bracelet begins to decrease symmetrically.

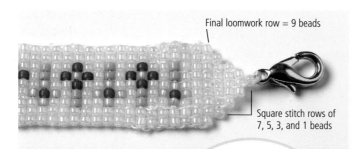

Final loomwork row = 9 beads

Square stitch rows of 7, 5, 3, and 1 beads

step 8

Continue decreasing until only one bead is left (see Decreasing, page 55). Attach the lobster clasp and split ring to the single beads at the ends of the bracelet by threading through the clasp/ring and around the single bead several times (see also Attaching clasps, page 98). Finish off the loose ends of thread (see Finishing off, page 83).

ADDING THE PICOT EDGE

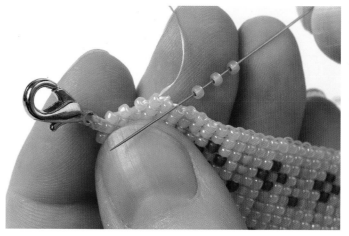

step 9
Bring the needle up through the last bead where the bracelet is at its full width. Thread on three pink seed beads, then pass the needle under the second loop of thread on the edge of the beadwork (see Picot edging on page 104, but note that this picot is being worked in a slightly different way).

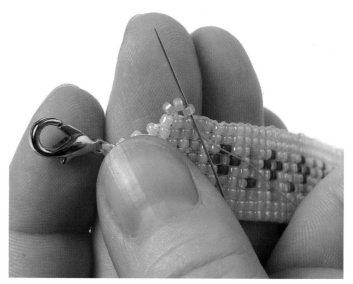

step 10
Bring the needle back up through the third picot bead just added.

step 11 Thread on two more pink seed beads and take the needle under the next loop of thread along the edge of the loomwork.

step 12 Bring the needle up through the second picot bead just added. Continue along the row in this way until the edge is complete. Repeat on the opposite side of the bracelet.

PRETTY PASTEL FLOWER MOTIFS ARE PERFECT FOR THIS FRIENDSHIP BRACELET, BUT YOU COULD CREATE A DIFFERENT DESIGN IF YOU PREFER. WHY NOT TRY A ZIGZAG DESIGN IN BRIGHT JAZZY COLORS, OR EXPERIMENT WITH AZTEC PATTERNS IN TERRACOTTAS AND BLUES?

Technique: HERRINGBONE STITCH

Herringbone stitch creates a wonderful chevron pattern when worked in both flat and tubular versions. Try experimenting with different shaped beads to create a variety of looks and textures. Herringbone stitch is usually worked with one strand of thread, but use two strands if you require a firm tension for items such as three-dimensional pieces.

Getting the tension right

It can take a while to master the tension of this stitch because the beads tend to move around. This is due mainly to the fact that the pairs you create on the row you are working are not actually linked together until the next row is added. If the tension is too loose, the beads will flop about, making it difficult to see where to make your next move. If the tension is too tight, the beads will buckle up and you will not achieve a chevron pattern. Practice makes perfect, so don't be put off—the results are well worth the effort.

STARTING THE BEADWORK

There are several ways to begin herringbone stitch, but a basic ladder is by far the easiest for a beginner.

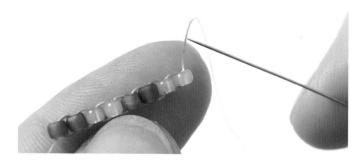

step 1 Make a ladder foundation in the same way as when starting brick stitch (see page 42). Eight beads will make a good-sized practice piece. Use pairs of beads in alternating colors to make it easy to see the emerging pattern.

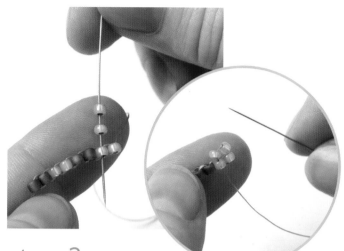

step 2 To begin row 2, pick up a pair of seed beads in the first color to match the pair of beads at the end of the ladder. Pass the needle down through the second bead on the ladder and gently pat the two new beads so that they sit side by side with the holes facing upward.

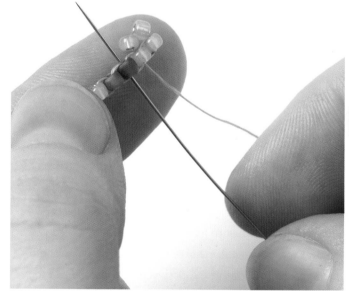

step 3 Bring the needle up through the third bead on the ladder row.

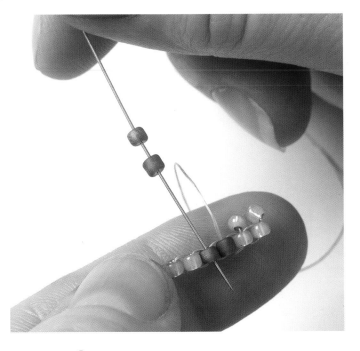

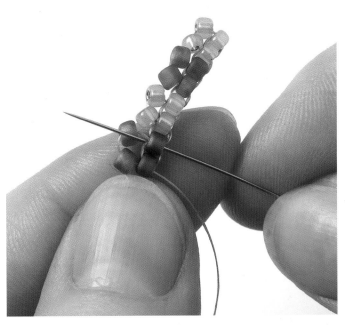

step 4 Thread on the next pair of beads, remembering to change color to match the pair below on the ladder row. Pass the needle down through the fourth bead along the ladder row. Pat the new pair of beads until they sit side by side with holes facing upward.

step 6 The working thread is now trailing from the first bead on the original ladder row, so you need to step up to the correct position to work another row. Start by taking the needle up through the second bead on the original ladder.

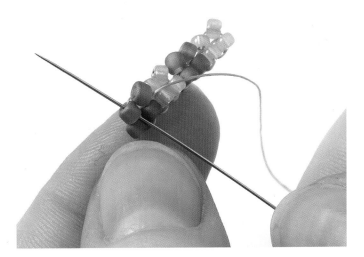

step 5 Continue adding pairs of beads along the row in this way. When the new row is complete, you will notice the herringbone or chevron effect starting to appear, with each pair of beads tilting slightly toward each other. At this point, the beads are sitting in matching pairs. The next row will connect the pairs together.

step 7 Now take the needle across and up through the first bead of the first pair on row 2.

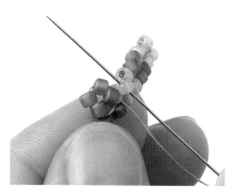

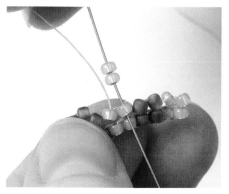

step 8 For row 3, thread on a pair of beads, then pass the needle down through the second bead on row 2.

step 9 Come up through the first bead of the next pair on row 2. This creates a linking stitch between each pair of beads on row 2.

step 10 Thread on two beads in the appropriate color and bring the needle down through the second bead of the pair below on row 2.

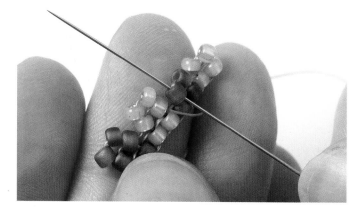

step 11 Pass the needle up through the first bead of the next pair on row 2. Continue adding pairs of beads along the row.

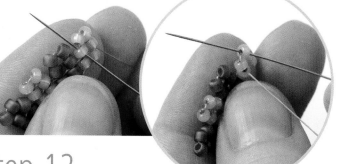

step 12 When you reach the end of row 3, step up to the correct position for row 4 by taking the needle back up through the second bead on row 2, then through the first bead of the first pair on row 3. You are now ready to begin row 4.

step 13 Continue adding rows in this way. As the beadwork grows, a wonderful chevron pattern emerges.

TUBULAR HERRINGBONE STITCH

Of all the beadworking techniques, this stitch produces one of the most attractive tubes, particularly when worked with triangle beads. The following steps are worked in two contrasting colors to enable you to see the rows clearly. Tubular herringbone stitch does slip and slide about at the start, but with a little perseverance you will create a great finished piece.

step 1 Make a foundation ladder row (see page 42) using six beads. Form a circle with the holes of the beads facing upward, then join the beads together by threading through the first and last beads on the ladder several times, ending with the thread emerging from the first bead.

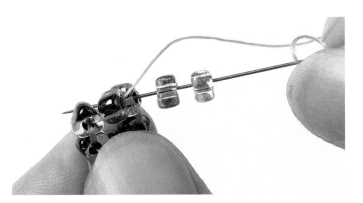

step 2 Thread on two beads in a contrasting color. Pass the needle down through the next bead on the ladder row, then thread up through the third bead on the ladder. Repeat to add two more pairs of beads.

step 3 To step up to the correct position for row 3, thread up through the next bead on the ladder row, then up through the first bead of the first pair on row 2.

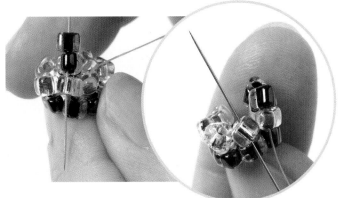

step 4 Pick up two beads and pass the needle down through the second bead of the first pair on row 2. Pass the needle up through the first bead of the next pair. This is the linking stitch.

step 5 Continue adding rows of tubular herringbone stitch until you reach the required length.

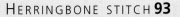

Project 14: METEOR SHOWER BRACELET

This is a great project to start your journey into herringbone stitch. The flat herringbone base has a lighter stripe running through the center to provide the perfect base for sparkling crystal accent beads. A classic bar clasp gives this cuff bracelet a classy finish.

MAKING THE BASE

4 black seed beads   2 white seed beads   4 black seed beads

step 1 Using four black, two white, and four black size 8 seed beads, make a ladder foundation row (see page 42).

step 2 Work a length of herringbone stitch (see page 90) to fit around the wrist, allowing about ⅝ in. (1.5 cm) for the clasp.

step 3 When you reach the other end of the bracelet, sew the pairs of beads into a ladder to match the start of the bracelet and to make attaching the clasp easier. Do this by passing the needle up and down through and between the pairs of beads in order to mirror the first end of the bracelet.

ADDING THE EMBELLISHMENT

step 4 It is best to leave
the first two rows of white beads at both ends of the bracelet
free from accent beads, which could interfere with the clasp.
Thread the needle down through the first two white beads on
the right-hand side at either end of the bracelet. Thread on a
drop bead, then pass the needle through the third white bead
on the left-hand side. This will make the drop bead sit between
the second and third pair of white beads in from the end of
the bracelet base.

step 5 Continue adding accent beads between the
rows of white seed beads. When attaching the crystals and star
beads, you will need to thread on the crystal or star and then
one size 15 black seed bead. Then, skipping the last seed bead,
thread the needle back through the crystal or star and into the
left-hand white bead on the bracelet base. The seed bead is
there to stop the accent bead from falling off the bracelet.

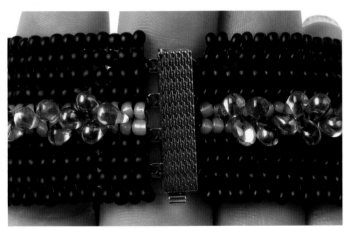

step 6 Attach the clasp to the ends of the bracelet (see
Bar clasps, page 100). Finish off the loose ends of thread (see
Finishing a thread, page 35).

SOME OF THE ACCENT BEADS HAVE
A SUBTLE IRIDESCENT FINISH TO ADD
AN EXTRA TOUCH OF SPARKLE TO
THIS SHIMMERING BRACELET.

Project 15: TUBULAR BRACELET

This design brings the traditional beaded bracelet up to date, creating a bangle effect. When you are wearing the bracelet, the light will catch the sides of the triangle beads beautifully. The finishing touch is the magnetic clasp surrounded by brick stitch, making the clasp look neat and tidy.

MAKING THE TUBE

step 1 Starting with either color of the triangle beads, make a ladder foundation row using six beads (see page 42). Join together into a circle with the bead holes all facing upward, then work a rope of tubular herringbone stitch (see page 93), alternating the colors of each row.

step 2 Continue until the bracelet has reached the required length, allowing about ⅝ in. (1.5 cm) for the clasp. When you have added the final row of beads, join the pairs of triangles together by threading up and down through and between the pairs to match the ladder at the start of the bracelet.

ATTACHING THE CLASP

step 3 Bring the needle through any of the end triangles, then thread one section of the clasp onto the needle. Pass the needle down through a triangle on the opposite side of the triangle circle.

step 4 As you pull the

thread through, center the clasp over the hole of the tube. Bring the needle up through the triangle next to the one you came down through. Thread the needle through the clasp once again, then back down through a triangle on the opposite side. Repeat this several times until the clasp feels secure.

step 6 Pass the
needle back up through the first seed bead, then down through the second seed bead, under the loop of thread, then back up through the second seed bead.

step 7 Now work brick stitch in the usual way, adding one seed bead at a time (see page 42). When you have beaded around to the start, take the needle back down through the first seed bead added, then up through the last bead added once again to secure. If needed, add a second row to cover the fixing point of the clasp. Repeat at the other end of the bracelet. Finish off the loose ends of thread (see Finishing a thread, page 35).

step 5 To add the wall of brick stitch around the base of the clasp, start by bringing the thread out of any of the triangles at the end of the bracelet. Pick up two seed beads, then pass the needle under the next loop of thread joining a pair of triangles.

A MONOCHROME COLOR SCHEME IS IDEAL FOR THIS BRACELET, ALLOWING THE CHEVRON STITCH PATTERN TO BECOME THE FOCAL POINT OF THE DESIGN.

Technique: ATTACHING CLASPS

Choosing an appropriate clasp can mean the success or failure of a finished piece of jewelry, so always buy the best clasp you can afford. Cheap clasps often tarnish or break easily, while more expensive clasps stand out from the crowd and really crown a piece. Learning how to attach a clasp in the correct manner is also important. It is worth taking your time and doing the job well.

SIMPLE CLASPS

Simple clasps, such as this inexpensive but highly decorative example, typically have one small fixing point at both sides. Adding a stem of a few small seed beads at each end of the beadwork will make the clasp easier to open and close.

Smaller beads
for flexible stem

step 1 Thread on three or four small seed beads at the end of the piece of beadwork where you want to attach the clasp. Thread the needle through the fixing point at one end of the clasp.

step 2 Thread the needle back through about five or six beads.

step 3 Tie a single knot between two beads at this point to allow you to turn the needle and thread it back up through the beads to the clasp.

step 4 Thread the needle through the clasp fixing point once again to give added strength. Repeat this journey once or twice until the clasp feels secure. Attach the other end of the beadwork to the other end of the clasp in the same way, remembering to add three or four small seed beads before the clasp. Finish off the loose ends of thread (see Finishing a thread, page 35).

TOGGLE CLASPS

A toggle clasp consists of a ring and a T-bar with a looped fixing point on each one. Always remember to add a stem of a few small seed beads at each end of the beadwork to make it easier to pass the T-bar through the ring.

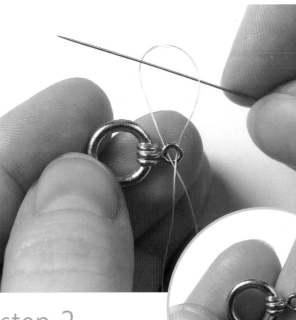

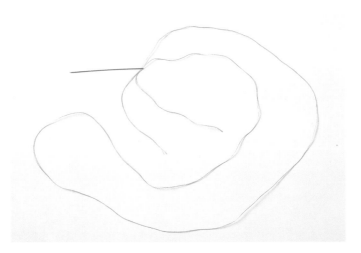

step 1 Using doubled thread will make it easier to attach the clasp and give the beadwork added strength. Pass both ends of a 5-ft. (1.5-m) length of thread through the eye of the needle.

step 2 Take the needle through the fixing point on the ring section of the clasp, leaving a loop of thread on the other side. Secure the thread by passing the needle through the loop. Pull the doubled thread firmly to secure it to the ring.

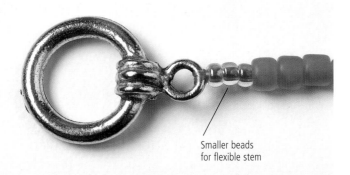

Smaller beads
for flexible stem

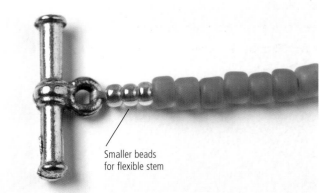

Smaller beads
for flexible stem

step 3 Thread on three or four small seed beads, then add enough beads to the core of the piece until you reach the required length.

step 4 Thread on another three or four small seed beads at the other end of the piece, attaching the T-bar section of the clasp in the same way as the ring section. Finish off the loose ends of thread (see Finishing a thread, page 35).

BAR CLASPS

These clasps are great for cuff bracelets and choker necklaces, because they are long and thin and keep wider sections of beadwork flat and in place. There is a wonderful array of bar clasps available, from plain and serviceable to more elaborate and ornate.

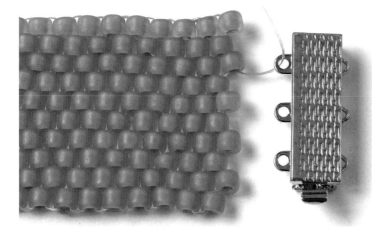

step 1 Place the bar clasp alongside the finished edge of the beadwork, aligning the beads to the clasp fixing points. Bring the needle out through one of the beads nearest to one of the fixing points on the clasp. Pass the needle through the corresponding fixing point on the clasp.

step 2 Thread the needle back through the bead in the main body of the beadwork. Repeat once or twice more until it feels secure.

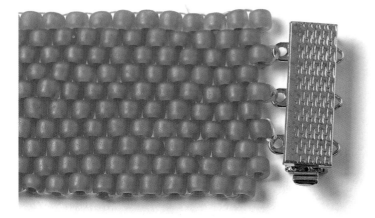

step 3 Repeat in the same way for the other fixing points on the clasp. Attach the other side of the clasp to the other end of the beadwork in the same way.

BEAD AND LOOP FASTENERS

Bead and loop fasteners are a very popular way of finishing off pieces of jewelry. They are one of the most discrete clasps because they can be constructed from the same beads used in the necklace or bracelet, making them an integral part of the piece.

Beads for fastening loop

Beads for stem

step 3 Add a stem of three or four small seed beads at the other end of the beadwork. Thread on more beads to make a loop large enough to slip over the bead fastener.

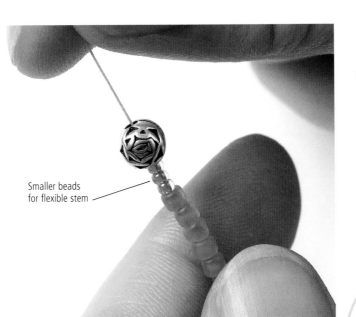

Smaller beads for flexible stem

step 1 Using a color that matches or complements the main beadwork, thread on three or four small seed beads to form a stem for the fastener bead. Thread on the fastener bead and push it down toward the small seed beads.

step 4 Pass the needle back down through the stem beads and into the main body of the work. Tie a single knot between two beads at this point to allow you to turn the needle and thread it back up through the stem and loop beads two or three more times for added security. Finish off the loose ends of thread (see Finishing a thread, page 35).

step 2 Thread on another small seed bead, then take the needle back down through the fastener bead, the three small seed beads, and into the main body of the beadwork. Tie a single knot between two beads at this point to allow you to turn the needle and thread it back up through the beads and around the fastener bead two or three more times until it feels secure.

Technique: DECORATIVE FINISHES

There are plenty of patterns, kits, and books available featuring wonderful beadwork designs. Here are a few decorative finishing techniques you can use to customize those designs. Never be afraid to add something extra—it could make your beadwork stand out from the crowd.

ADDING A FRINGE

Beads drape beautifully when strung as a fringe and look great on almost any beaded piece. You can also create patterns within the fringe to extend the design from the main beadwork into it. Decide whether you want the fringe to be straight or worked into a central point. If the latter, it is best to place the central fringe first and then work outward, first to one side and then the other. If you work from one end to the other, by the time you reach the center you may find that the central fringe is too long.

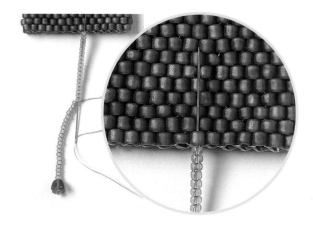

step 2 Skipping the last bead added, thread the needle back through the accent bead and then through all the remaining beads on the fringe. Pass the needle back up through the bead you initially emerged from in the main body of the beadwork.

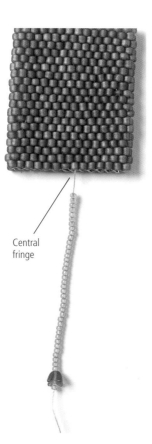

Central fringe

step 1 The best way to center a fringe is to fold the piece in half and place a needle through the central bead. Attach a new 5-ft. (1.5-m) length of beading thread near to where the first fringe is to be placed. Weave the needle up and down the beads until the thread is coming out of the bead that will hold the fringe. Thread on the required number of beads, in this instance seed beads, and slide them down toward the main beadwork. Add an accent bead if required, followed by an extra seed bead.

step 3 Thread the needle down through the next bead, ready to add the second strand of fringing. Add all the remaining fringes in the same way.

BEADER'S TIP

If you are planning to add a pattern to the fringe, figure out the design on graph paper first using colored pencils. As you add each fringe, hold the work up to check that the pattern is correct and that each strand is hanging in the right position. If the fringe is too loose, the beads will not sit snugly. If the fringe is too tight, the beads will buckle and the fringe will not drape well.

BRANCH FRINGING

Branch fringing is a great way of adding color, shape, and texture to a piece. This can be achieved by using different sizes of beads together with dynamic accent beads.

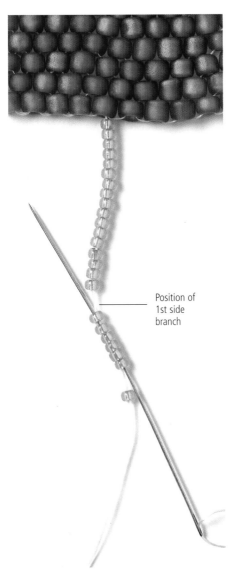

Position of 1st side branch

step 1
Add the first strand of fringing in the usual way. Skipping the last bead added, pass the needle back up through the beads, with the needle emerging where you wish to position the first side branch.

step 2
Thread on the required number of beads for the branch. Skipping the last bead added, thread back up through the beads of the branch.

Position of 2nd side branch

step 3
Pass the needle back into the main strand of fringing and take it through the beads to the place where you wish to add the second side branch.

step 4
Add as many side branches as you wish, then take the needle back up through the remaining beads on the central fringe and up through two or three beads on the main piece of beadwork. Turn the needle and bring it back down through the beadwork to the position where you want to place the next fringe.

PICOT EDGING

Picot edging is great fun to do and can be added to almost anything. Several different effects can be achieved, depending on how many beads are used for each picot and where they are placed. If three beads are used, they will gather into little points and look very effective when the central bead is a different color to accentuate the point. If more beads are used for the picots, they look like little frills. Picots can be added to necklaces, bracelets, earrings, and amulet purses—the possibilities are endless.

step 2 Thread on three beads.

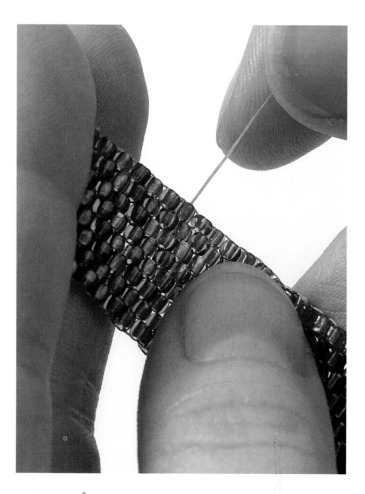

step 1 Bring the needle out of the main body of the beadwork at the point where you wish to add a picot.

step 3 Pass the needle down through the next bead along on the main beadwork.

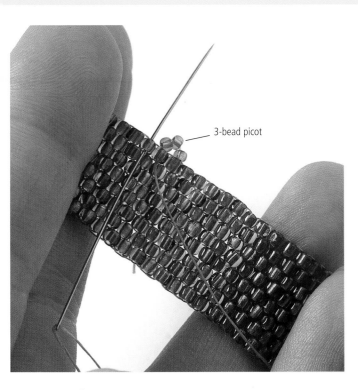

3-bead picot

step 4 Thread the needle up through the next bead along on the main beadwork, making sure that the first picot is pulled up to the beadwork.

step 5 Thread on three more beads to create the next picot. Continue adding as many picots as required.

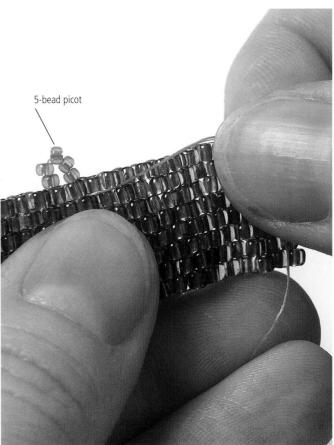

5-bead picot

step 6 Here, five beads are added to create a different effect—a frill rather than a point.

BEADED LOOPS

Beaded loops are another great decorative addition to any
beadwork project. Simple and fairly quick to do, they give
instant impact to any piece.

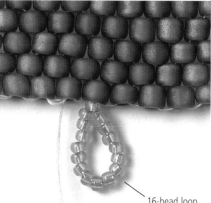

1st bead

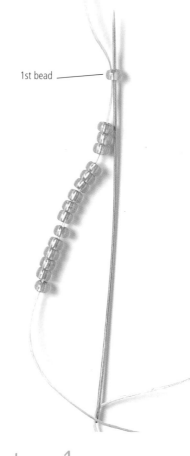

16-bead loop

step 2 Pull the thread through
the first bead to form a loop.

step 3 Take the needle back
up into the main body of the beadwork.
Turn the needle and bring it back down
through the beadwork to the position
where you want to place the next
beaded loop.

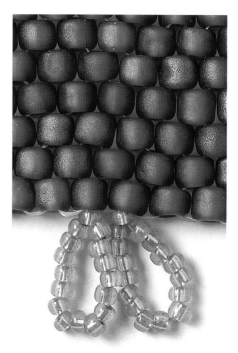

step 4 Keep
adding bead loops where
required until the design
is complete. Remember
to pull each loop up
every time a new loop
is formed or you risk
finding unsightly loose
threads when the design
is finished.

step 1 Bring the needle out
of the main piece of beadwork at the
place where you wish to position a
beaded loop. Thread on the number of
beads for the size of loop you require,
then pass the needle back through the
first bead added.

STRUNG LOOPS

This is another simple but effective way of creating a decorative edge, using strings of beads to form shallow loops. In this example, strings of 10 size 11 beads are looped at intervals of 4 beads along the main piece of beadwork.

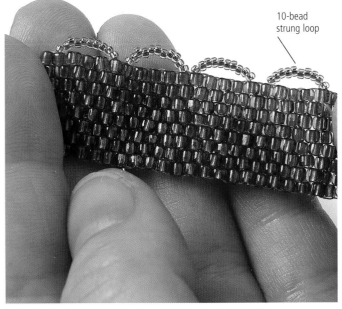

10-bead strung loop

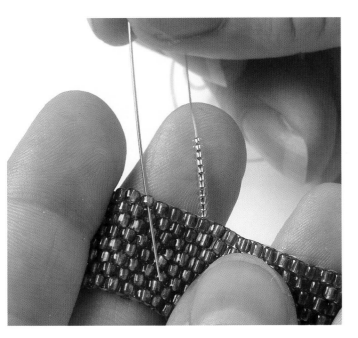

step 1 Bring the needle out through the main piece of beadwork where you wish to add a string of beads. Thread on 10 beads, then count along 3 beads on the edge of the beadwork, taking the needle down through the 4th bead.

step 3 Continue adding strings of beads along the row until complete, leaving three beads between each string.

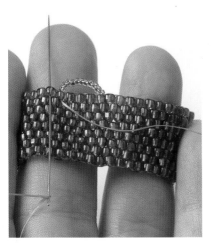

step 2 Pass the needle up through the fifth bead, ready to add the next loop.

Overlapping strung loops

step 4 If you wish, you can make a return journey along the edge, placing a string of beads between each of the initial loops added. Start by bringing the needle up through the central bead of the three beads missed between the ends of the first loop. Thread on 10 beads and make another strung loop. Continue all along the edge.

Technique: WIREWORK

Once you enter the world of wire jewelry, the possibilities are endless. So much of the fashion jewelry available today is created using wire as its base. When first using this technique, it is best to choose a very simple project to help build your confidence. The wirework earrings and bracelet on pages 110 and 112 are both suitable for learning basic wirework skills. There are many different tools and materials available for wirework, from wire jigs to coiling gizmos, but only a few items are essential.

Wire

The choice of wire is endless. Most inexpensive wire is plated, which means that the base metal is usually nickel, copper, or aluminum, with a coating to give it the same look as precious metal. Also available are many colored wires. These are coated with either enamel or nylon, and are great for fashion work. However, over long periods of time the color will wear off. When you first start to work with wire, use manageable lengths of no more than 12 in. (30 cm). This will stop the wire from kinking and looking worn.

Metal chains

Chains are available in both precious and plated metals. They form an ideal base for necklaces and bracelets, allowing you to attach your favorite beads to them using pieces of wire, jump rings, or headpins. When choosing a chain, you will need to match the size of the links to the gauge of the wire you will be using with them. Also think about your budget, since chains can be expensive.

WIRE SIZES

When you first go to purchase wire, it can be very confusing. Some companies label their wire in gauges, while others use millimeters. Use the conversion chart below to help when you are selecting wire to buy.

Gauge size	Millimeters
32	0.2 mm
28	0.3 mm
26	0.4 mm
24	0.5 mm
22	0.6 mm
20	0.8 mm
18	1.0 mm
16	1.3 mm
14	1.6 mm

Wire This is now available in many fabulous colors, widths, and configurations.

Metal chains Chains are available in many different shapes and sizes, ranging from precious metals to inexpensive craft chains.

Essential pliers

When choosing pliers, buy the best you can afford. It is a good idea to keep your tools in a case away from dampness, which may cause them to go rusty.

Flush cutters These do exactly as they their name implies—they cut wire, leaving a clean, wedge-shaped end. They have a small point, enabling you to reach into tight spaces—a must for the wireworker.

Round nose pliers These are the most important pliers for wirework, and are used to create all the loops.

Chain nose pliers These are used for opening and closing small chain links, hence their name. They have no teeth, so they will not mark or make any unwanted impressions in your work.

BEADER'S TIP

If you are just starting wirework, it is a good idea not to spend too much on your first few reels of wire. You then will not feel quite so bad when discarding sections of wire that have not gone exactly to plan. Wirework is all about practice. The more you handle the wire and tools, the better you will become. Don't strive for perfection in your early pieces—it is the overall look that matters. It is a good idea to practice bending and twisting the wire into loops, wrapped loops, and S-bends. You will notice that the wire becomes smoother and less kinked as you get used to working with it.

Holding pliers

Position the pliers in the palm of your hand, with one side of the pliers running alongside the ball of your thumb, and the other side of the pliers running along the length of your fingers.

Project 16: BEAD-AND-WIRE EARRINGS

A great introduction to working with beads and wire is to make drop earrings using ready-made components such as headpins and earring posts. This project is ideal for using up leftover beads from larger projects. They also make great gifts for family and friends.

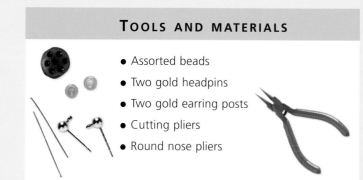

MAKING THE EARRINGS

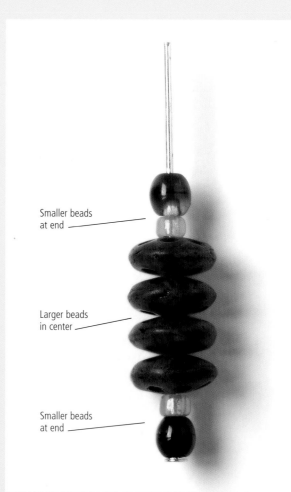

Smaller beads at end

Larger beads in center

Smaller beads at end

step 2 Use cutting pliers to trim off the excess wire, making sure that you leave about ⅜ in. (1 cm) of spare wire to finish off the earring. If you are new to working with wire, it is a good idea to leave slightly more than you need. Remember that you can always cut off a little more later if you need to.

step 1 Thread the beads in the required order onto the headpins. If you are incorporating one or more larger beads into the design, it is a good idea to flank them on both sides with smaller beads. This gives a good balance to the design.

step 3 Hold the bead drop between your thumb and fingertips. Position the round nose pliers slightly above where the beads are lying on the wire. Bend the wire toward you.

step 4 Move the pliers to the top of the wire and use their tips to roll the wire around to form a loop. If you find that the loop is too large, unroll the loop slightly, cut off another section of wire, and then reroll the loop.

step 5 If the loop looks a little messy, reinsert the pliers and use them to shape the loop more neatly, using a smooth rolling action.

YOU CAN USE ANY COMBINATION OF BEADS YOU LIKE TO CREATE DROP EARRINGS, FROM A SINGLE LARGE BEAD TO THE MULTIPLE BEAD DESIGN SHOWN HERE.

step 6 When you are happy with the loop, use the round nose pliers to reopen the loop enough to slip on the earring post. Reclose the loop using the pliers as before. Make a matching earring in the same way.

Project 17: WIREWORK CHARM BRACELET

This bracelet proves that you do not have to spend a fortune to create the latest fashionable look. It is the clever use of color, shape, and texture that gives the bracelet its impact.

MAKING THE BRACELET

step 1 Using cutting pliers, cut a length of chain for the bracelet, allowing about ⅝ in. (1.5 cm) for the clasp.

step 2 Add a jump ring to one end of the chain. First, open the jump ring by twisting it apart using two pairs of pliers. Do not pull the ring apart; instead, twist one pair of pliers toward you, and the other away from you. This opens the jump ring correctly without putting any strain on the wire, and makes it easier to close up again. Slip the ring through the last link at one end of the chain, then twist it closed.

step 3 Open a second jump ring and slip it through the last link at the other end of the chain. Slip the lobster clasp onto the ring as well, and then twist the ring closed.

EMBELLISHING THE BRACELET

step 4 Add the charms first, spacing them evenly along the bracelet. Do this using jump rings in the same way as you attached the lobster clasp.

step 6 Continue adding bead-and-wire drops in this way until you are happy with the finished result. It is worth making a few different drops and experimenting with them, fixing them to the bracelet to see how they look. Remember that they are relatively easy to remove and reposition.

step 5 Now add the bead-and-wire drops by threading beads onto gold headpins and then looping the end of each pin around a link in the bracelet chain (see Bead-and-wire earrings, page 110).

THE GOLD CHARMS AND CHAIN COMPLEMENT EACH OTHER, WHILE THE BEADS ADD COLOR TO THE DESIGN. BRIGHT RED ACCENT BEADS ADD VIBRANCY TO THE COLOR SCHEME.

Project 18: RETRO FLOWER PIN

This retro-inspired pin can be completed relatively quickly and is great fun to make. Wiring accent beads and seed bead leaves onto a mesh pin base is really easy to do.

TOOLS AND MATERIALS

- 10 g size 11 seed beads: bright pink
- 10 g size 11 seed beads: pale pink
- 10 g size 11 seed beads: burgundy
- 8 leaf accent beads: green
- Small flower accent beads: pink
- Medium flower accent beads: pink
- Mesh pin
- Beading wire
- Cutting pliers
- Flat nose pliers

MAKING THE PETALS

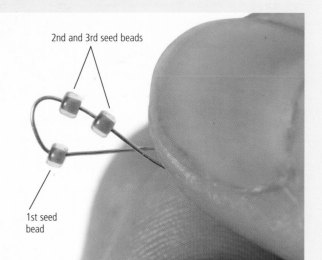

2nd and 3rd seed beads

1st seed bead

step 1 Use cutting pliers, cut a 12-in. (30-cm) length of beading wire. Make a bright pink petal by threading three seed beads onto the wire. Bend the wire in half and position the first seed bead to one side of the bend and the other two beads to the other side.

step 2 Pass the end of the wire where the first bead is sitting through the other two beads to form a loop. Use flat nose pliers to pull the wire all the way through until the beads sit close together in a triangular formation.

step 3 Thread three more beads onto either end of the wire. Push them up next to the first three beads and bend the wire around so that the three beads just added sit neatly underneath the two above. Pass the other end of the wire through the beads just added, so that there are two ends of wire running through them.

step 4
Continue adding rows of beads in this way, increasing one bead each time. When you have reached eight beads in width, decrease one bead each time until you are down to two beads. This is the end of the petal that will be attached to the pin base.

Work 8 of these

Work 2 of these

Work 2 of these

step 5
Work a second bright pink petal with a central row of eight beads, eight pale pink petals with a central row of seven beads, and two burgundy petals with a central row of eight beads.

WIRING THE ACCENT BEADS

step 6
Cut several 4-in. (10-cm) lengths of beading wire. The leaves used here have horizontal (top-drilled) holes, so the wire is threaded through the holes. Cross the two ends and twist them around each other once. If your flowers have vertical (center-drilled) holes like those used here, thread one end of wire up through the flower halfway, add any color seed bead, and then thread the other end of the wire up through the flower. Twist the wire to hold it in place as before. The number of accent beads you need will depend on the size of the mesh pin.

ASSEMBLING THE PIN

step 7
Attach the seed bead petals by passing the wire down through the front of the mesh section of the pin in the second row of holes from the outer edge. Twist the wires around each other on the back of the mesh to secure the petal in place. Flatten the wire down and trim the ends to about 1 in. (2.5 cm).

step 8
Continue to attach the petals in a pleasing design. Attach the accent beads to the center of the mesh in the same way, making sure that you cover any gaps. Attach the mesh section to the pin back by clamping the holding bars into place using flat nose pliers.

THE DIFFERENT TONES OF COLOR IN THE FLOWER BEADS ARE ECHOED IN THE BEADED PETALS TO CREATE A HARMONIOUS DESIGN.

Technique: STRINGING

Sometimes when you find some beautiful beads, all you need to do is thread them together in a string to create a truly unfussy look that will display the beads to their best potential. You can string the beads on a variety of different materials, including beading wire, memory wire, suede, leather, and ribbon. The only real skill required is to learn how to finish the ends of the threading material.

SIMPLE STRINGING

This is a quick and easy way of creating a bracelet or necklace using plastic-coated beading wire with knot cups and a clasp.

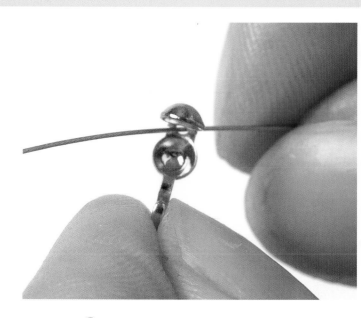

step 2 Pass one end of the wire through the hinge of the knot cup.

step 1 Lay out your chosen beads and try several different arrangements until you are happy with the look. Cut the required length of plastic-coated beading wire, allowing an extra 6 in. (15 cm) for the knot cups and clasp. Thread the beads onto the wire.

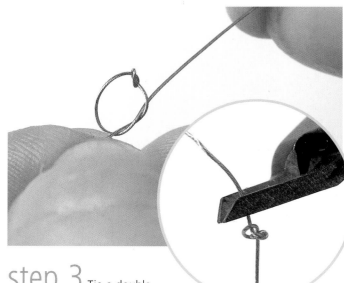

step 3 Tie a double knot at the point you wish the knot cup to sit, remembering to leave enough wire on the other side to finish. Using cutting pliers, trim the wire close to the double knot, then put a dab of clear nail polish over the knot.

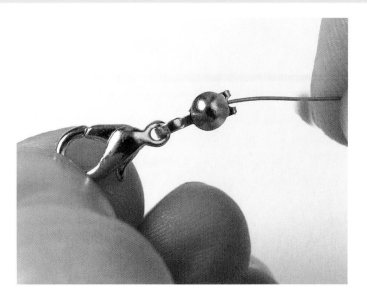

step 5 Slip a lobster clasp onto the open loop of the knot cup. Using round nose pliers, close the loop. Repeat at the other end of the wire, adding a knot cup and a jump ring or split ring.

step 4 Pull the thread through the knot cup until the knot sits neatly inside. Using round nose pliers, gently close the knot cup.

SIMPLY STRINGING BEADS ONTO WIRE IS A GREAT WAY TO DISPLAY BEADS TO THEIR BEST EFFECT. CHOOSE WITH A SIMPLE CLASP RATHER THAN A MORE ELABORATE ONE SO THAT YOU DO NOT DETRACT ANY ATTENTION AWAY FROM THE BEADS.

Using memory wire

If you want to create almost instant chokers and bracelets, memory wire is the medium to work with. The wire remains in a coil even after beads have been added, hence its name. It is tough and durable, and a great way to introduce children to beading. Use strong wire cutters to cut the required amount of memory wire. Never use a delicate pair because they will be ruined by the wire.

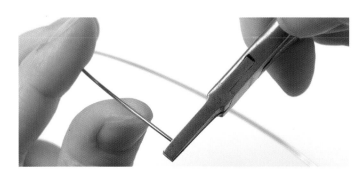

step 1 Place one end of the memory wire between the jaws of a pair of flat nose pliers.

step 3 Using the unbent end of the memory wire as a needle, thread on the beads until only about ¼ in. (6 mm) of wire is unbeaded. Bend this end of the wire over to form a loop, as before, to finish the piece.

step 2 Bend the wire downward, then bend the wire back on itself to form a loop.

MEMORY WIRE IS THICKER THAN BEADING WIRE, AND IT LOOKS BEST WHEN ENTIRELY COVERED WITH BEADS. SIMPLY OPEN UP THE CIRCLE TO SLIP IT ONTO YOUR NECK OR WRIST, THEN ALLOW THE WIRE TO SPRING BACK INTO ITS CIRCULAR SHAPE.

BEADER'S TIP

Add a central pendant to memory wire chokers by hanging the pendant from a jump ring at the center of the beaded wire. Instead of finishing the ends by bending the wire to form a loop that will stop the beads from escaping, as shown here, you can buy half-drilled beads to glue onto the ends of the wire.

USING FLAT LEATHER CRIMPS

Large beads can be threaded onto suede, leather, or ribbon.
These necklaces or chokers can simply be tied at the back of the
neck, but a more professional look can be obtained with the use
of flat leather crimps on each end of the material. When these
are secured, attach a lobster clasp and jump ring to the ends
of the flat leather crimps.

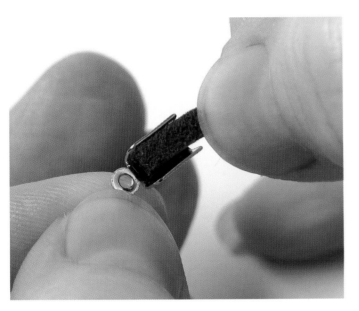

step 2 Using round
nose pliers, bend one side of the
crimp over. Reposition the pliers to
bend the other side over so that it sits on top
of the first side, trapping the material inside.

step 1 Place the cord into the flat leather crimp so that
the end of the cord aligns with the end of the crimp.

step 3 Open a jump ring using
two pairs of pliers, such as round nose
and flat nose pliers (see page 112). Slide the
jump ring through the loop of the crimp. Slip a
lobster clasp onto the jump ring, then use the pliers
to close the jump ring. Add a jump ring to the other flat leather
crimp to complete the fastening.

You do not have to be an accomplished knitter to create bead-and-wire jewelry. Only basic knitting skills are required, all of which are explained here. As a general rule, 0.2 or 0.3 mm wire is the easiest to knit with. Work a small section to test if the wire is suitable for knitting. If it is too fine, the wire will snap; if it is too thick, it will be almost impossible to knit with. Bamboo needles are best because the wire does not slip about quite as much as when worked on aluminum needles. Size 0–2 (2–2.75 mm) needles are a good size for working with 0.2 mm wire, and size 6 (4 mm) for 0.3 mm wire. However, it really depends on the effect you want to achieve. You could use bamboo skewers if you do not have any knitting needles.

Getting the tension right

The tension (usually referred to as gauge in knitting) has to be correct from the start because it is difficult to adjust afterward. You need to keep the wire quite loopy on the needles to enable you to form stitches easily. Work a test piece to see whether you need to adjust your tension before knitting the main piece.

WIRE KNITTING LOOKS VERY MESSY TO START WITH, BUT KEEP GOING AND YOU WILL SOON SEE GREAT RESULTS. THIS BRACELET HAS BEEN FINISHED WITH A PAIR OF TOGGLE CLASPS (SEE PAGE 107).

step 1 Thread about 10 g of beads directly onto the spool of beading wire without cutting it. Keep pushing the beads down toward the spool end of the wire.

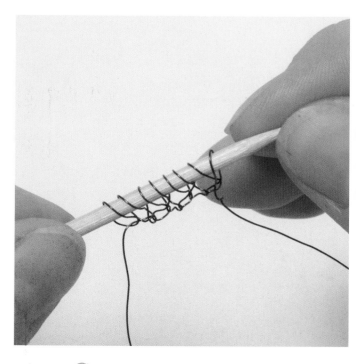

step 2 Cast on the number of stitches required for your design (see box, opposite, for a simple cast-on technique). As a rough guide, eight stitches will produce a 2-in. (5-cm) wide section of knitting.

KNITTING SKILLS: CASTING ON

Casting on is the process of making your first row of stitches on the knitting needle. There are several different ways of casting on; the thumb method shown here is the simplest.

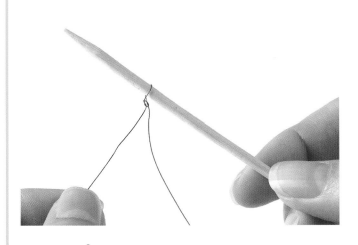

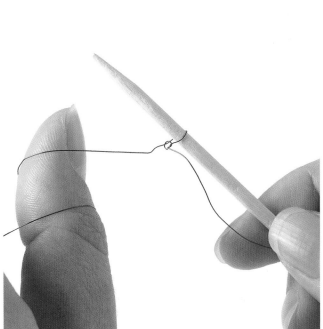

step A Wrap one end of the wire around the needle and make a slip knot, leaving a 6-in. (15-cm) tail of wire. This forms the first stitch.

step B Hold the needle in one hand and grip the working end of the wire with the fingers of your other hand. Wrap the wire around your thumb to form a loop.

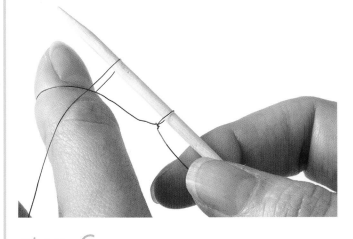

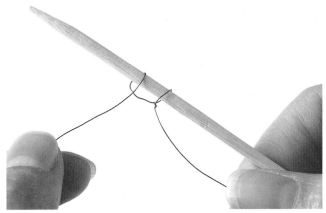

step C Push the tip of the needle up through the loop on your thumb.

step D Slip your thumb out of the loop and gently pull the working end of the wire to tighten the new stitch on the needle, remembering to keep it fairly loopy. Repeat this process to cast on as many stitches as required.

step 3 Knit three rows (see box, right) without any beads.

step 4 Knit the first stitch of row 4 in the usual way, then push several beads up into the palm of the hand holding the working end of the wire. Remember to keep the tension of the wire loose.

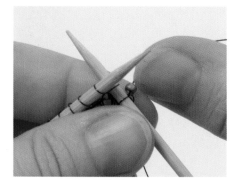

step 5 As you are about to knit the second stitch, push a bead up behind the crossed needles, ready to be knit into the wire. Knit the second stitch in the usual way.

KNITTING SKILLS: KNIT STITCH

The knit stitch is the most basic stitch used to make a knit fabric and is very easy to master. Hold the needle with the cast-on stitches in your left hand and the empty needle in your right hand.

step A Insert the right needle into the center of the first stitch from front to back so that the two needles cross each other with the right needle behind. Make sure that the working end of the wire is behind the needles.

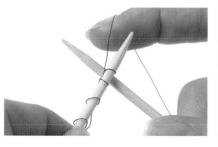

step B Using an index finger, wrap the working end of the wire counterclockwise around the tip of the right needle.

step C Use the right needle to pull the wrapped wire through the stitch on the left needle to create a new stitch on the right needle.

step D Slip the original stitch off the left needle, then continue knitting along the row in this way.

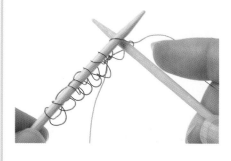

step E Swap the needles at the end of each row so that you begin the new row holding the needle with the stitches in your left hand and the empty needle in your right hand.

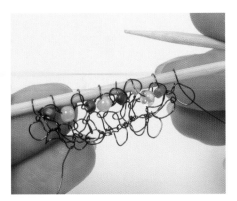

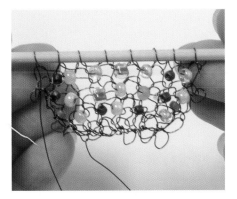

step 6
Continue along the row, knitting a bead into each stitch until you reach the final stitch. Knit this stitch without a bead. If you included a bead in the end stitches, they would stick out through the side of the work.

step 7
Work a row without adding any beads. This does two things—it makes the beads go farther and gives you a flat side that will sit comfortably against the skin.

step 8
Continue alternating beaded and unbeaded rows until the required length is reached. Work three unbeaded rows to match the first end of the knitting, then bind off (see box, below). Finish off the wire ends by winding the wire around itself to secure, making sure there are no sharp edges.

KNITTING SKILLS: BINDING OFF
When you have finished the knitting, you need to bind off to make a neat edge that does not unravel.

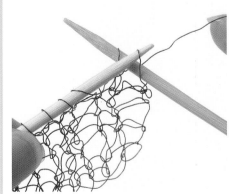

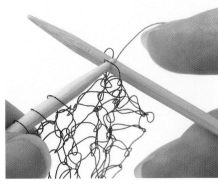

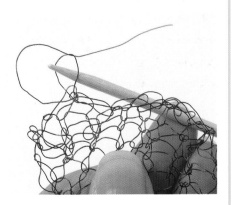

step A
Knit the first two stitches in the usual way. Insert the tip of the left needle into the first of these knit stitches.

step B
Lift this stitch over the second stitch and slip it off the right needle so that you have only one stitch on the right needle. Knit the next stitch on the left needle so that there are two stitches on the right needle once again. Lift the first of these stitches over the second stitch and slip it off the right needle as before.

step C
Continue binding off stitches in this way until the end of the row. Cut off the wire, leaving a 6-in. (15-cm) tail. Thread the tail through the last stitch, remove the needle, and tighten.

RESOURCES

Bead Societies

There are bead societies throughout North America—just contact your local library for details. Alternatively, a quick Internet search will produce a list of possible societies and groups.

Austin Bead Society

P.O. Box 656

Austin, TX 78767-0656

austinbeadsociety@yahoo.com

www.austinbeadsociety.org

Baltimore Bead Society

8510 High Ridge Road

Ellicott City, MD 21043

baltbead@bcpl.net

www.baltobead.org

The Bead Museum

5754 West Glenn Drive

Glendale, AZ 85301

www.thebeadmuseum.com

Bead Society of Calgary

#507–320 Meredith Road Northeast

Calgary, Alberta T2E 5A6

The Bead Society of Greater Chicago

P.O. Box 8103

Wilmette, IL 60091-8103

www.bsgc.org

The Bead Society of Greater New York

P.O. Box 6219

FDR Station

New York, NY 10150

info@nybead.org

www.nybead.org

Bead Society of Greater Vancouver

Richmond Arts Center

7700 Minoru Gate

Vancouver, British Columbia V6B 3A0

The Bead Society of Greater Washington

The Jennifer Building

400 Seventh Street Northwest

Washington, DC 20004

info@beadmuseumdc.org

www.bsgw.org

The Bead Society of Los Angeles

P.O. Box 241874

Los Angeles, CA 90024

info@beadsocietyla.org

www.beadsocietyla.org

Bead Society of New Hampshire

P.O. Box 3535

Concord, NH 03301

gdevoid@tds.net

www.beadsocietyof newhampshire.org

The Bead Society of Orange County

2202 Main Street

Santa Ana, CA 92706

corliss@media-enterprises.com

www.beadsocietyoc.org

Cumberland Valley Bead Society

P.O. Box 41903

Nashville, TN 37204

motherbead@aol.com

www.cvbeads.net

Great Lakes Beadworkers Guild

P.O. Box 1639

Royal Oak, MI 48068-1639

webmaster@greatlakes beadworkersguild.org

www.greatlakes beadworkersguild.org

Bead Society of Hawaii-Maui

P.O. Box 12127

Lahaina

Maui, HI 96761

International Society of Glass Beadmakers

1120 Chester Avenue #470

Cleveland, OH 44114

www.isgb.org

Madison Bead Society

P.O. Box 620383

Middleton, WI 53562-0383

madisonbeadsoc@hotmail.com

www.madisonbeadsociety.org

National Bead Society

3855 Lawrenceville Highway

Lawrenceville, GA 30044

www.nationalbeadsociety.com

Niagara Bead Society

8 Drayton Court

St. Catharines, Ontario L2N 5R9

http://niagara.cioc.ca/details.asp?RSN=6746&Number=0

Northwest Bead Society

P.M.B. 564

4616 25th Avenue Northeast

Seattle, WA 98105

www.nwbeadsociety.org

Oklahoma Bead Society

5144 S New Haven Avenue

Tulsa, OK 74135

www.okbeadsociety.com

Portland Bead Society

P.O. Box 997

Portland, OR 97207-0997

president@beadport.com

www.beadport.com

Rocky Mountain Bead Society

P.O. Box 480721

Denver, CO 80248-0721

rmbs@rockybeads.org

www.rockybeads.org

Saginaw Valley Bead Society

926 Reed Street

Saginaw, MI 48602

www.saginawvalleybeadsociety.org

San Antonio Bead and Ornament Society

P.O. Box 100113

San Antonio, TX 78201

sabostx@hotmail.com

www.sabostx.com

South Jersey Bead Society

P.O. Box 1365

Merchantville, NJ 08109

www.southjerseybeadsociety.org

Spokane-Northwest Bead Society

P.O. Box 40225

Mead, WA 99021

Toronto Bead Society

233–253 College Street

Toronto, Ontario M5T 1R5

info@torontobeadsociety.org

www.torontobeadsociety.org

Upper Midwest Bead Society

3000 University Avenue Southeast, #5

Minneapolis, MN 55414

http://umbeads.tripod.com

Wild West Bead Society

1009 Ridgetop Drive

Justin, TX 76247-4261

info@wildwestbeadsociety.com

www.wildwestbeadsociety.com

Wyoming TumbleBeaders Bead Society

P.O. Box 1431

Cheyenne, WY 82003-1431

wyotumblebeaders@yahoo.com

www.geocities.com/wyotumblebeaders

Suppliers

Addiction Beads

2256 Bromsgrove Road

Mississauga, Ontario L5J 4A3

www.addictionbeads.com

Beads, kits, and general jewelry-making supplies.

Atlantic Gems

8609 Second Avenue

#103B Silver Spring, MD 20910

(401) 624-4332

www.atlanticgems.com

Findings, tools, Swarovski crystals, and many other beads.

Auntie's Beads

4113 West 83rd Street

Prairie Village, KS 66208

(913) 642-7092

www.auntiesbeads.com

Beads, tools, clasps, and general beading supplies.

Beadcats

PO Box 2840

Wilsonville, OR 97070-2840

(503) 625-2323

www.beadcats.com

Beads, books, and general jewelry-making supplies.

Bead Connections

#122–4th Avenue

Kamloops, British Columbia V2C 3N4

(800) 260-9295

www.beadlady.net

Quality beads and crystals.

Bead Creative

5401 Sheridan Drive

Williamsville, NY 14221

(716) 626-4182

www.beadcreative.com

Beads, tools, threads, and kits.

The Beading Room

GTA, Toronto

Ontario M4M 2M8

(416) 462-9102

www.thebeadingroom.com

Online source for beads, tools, and general beading supplies.

Beads Galore

2123 South Priest, Suite 201

Tempe, AZ 85282

(480) 921-3949

www.beadsgalore.com

Glass and metal beads, Swarovski crystals, and beading supplies.

Beadworks

149 Washington Street

Norwalk, CT 06854

(203) 852-9194

www.beadworks.com

Wide selection of beads in many materials, including gemstone, metal, glass, plastic, and porcelain.

Corbeeta

32445 Marshall Road

Abbotsford

British Columbia V2T 1A7

(778) 552-1874

http://corbeeta.com

Beads, findings, Swarovski crystals, and general beading supplies.

Crystal Beads of Boston

31 Hayward Street, Suite A-1

Franklin, MA 02038

(866) 702-3237

www.crystalbeadsofboston.com

Swarovski crystals and pearls.

The eBead Store

R R #3 Warkworth, Ontario K0K 3K0

(705) 924-3903

www.theebeadstore.com

Beads and jewelry supplies.

Fire Mountain Gems

One Fire Mountain Way

Grants Pass, OR 97526-2373

(800) 355-2137

www.firemountaingems.com

Large selection of beads, including semiprecious stones, and general beading supplies.

Marsha Neal Studio

P.O. Box 1560

Hockessin, DE 19707

(302) 559-6781

www.marshanealstudio.com

Ceramic pendants.

The Natural Bead

357 Brant Street

Burlington, Ontario L7R 2G9

(905) 681-9249

www.thenaturalbead.com

Beads from around the world.

Out on a Whim

121 East Cotati Avenue

Cotati, CA 94931

(800) 232-3111

www.whimbeads.com

Seed beads and general beading supplies.

Pacific Silverworks

461E Main Street, Suite A

Ventura, CA 93001

(805) 641-1394

www.pacificsilverworks.com

High-quality silver findings.

Shipwreck Beads

8560 Commerce Place Drive N.E.

Dept B1 Lacey, WA 98516

(800) 950-4232

www.shipwreckbeads.com

Large selection of beads, including Czech fire-polished beads and Swarovski crystals.

Wild About Beads

436 Main Road

Tiverton, RI 02878

(401) 624-4332

www.wildaboutbeads.com

Many types of beads, including custom handmade beads. Also general jewelry-making supplies.

Worldly Treasures

1226 Washington Street

Mainitowoc, WI 54220

(920) 686-2323

www.worldlytreasures.biz

Handcrafted beads in natural materials, including shell and pearl.

Wynwoods Gallery and Bead Studio

940 Water Street

Port Townsend, WA 98368

(888) 311-6131

www.wynwoodds.com

Beads, charms, and general supplies.

Web Sites

www.beadandbutton.com

The Web site for *Bead & Button* magazine.

www.beadexpo.com

An annual conference and bazaar.

www.beadingtimes.com

An online beading magazine.

http://beadwork.about.com

There is an active forum and plenty of links and articles on this site.

www.interweave.com/bead

The Web site for *Beadwork* magazine.

www.members.cox.net/sdsantan/beadfairies.html

A useful resources site with lots of links and tips.

INDEX

CREDITS

Many thanks to The Bead Scene for supplying all the beads and
equipment used in this book.

The Bead Scene
P.O. Box 6351
Towcester
Northamptonshire NN12 7YX
+44 (0)1327 811-101
Stephanie@thebeadscene.com
www.thebeadscene.com

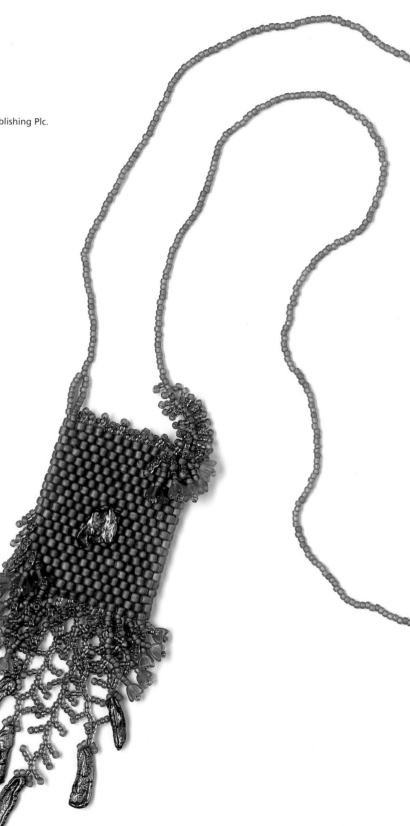